Soccer:

A Step-by-Step Guide on How to Stop the Other Team, About Each Player on a Team, and How to Lead Your Players, Manage Parents, and Select the Best Formation

Dylan Joseph

Soccer:
A Step-by-Step Guide on How to Stop the Other Team, About
Each Player on a Team, and How to Lead Your Players,
Manage Parents, and Select the Best Formation
By: Dylan Joseph

WAIT!

Wouldn't it be nice to have the steps in this book on an easy four-page printout for you to take to the field? Well, here is your chance!

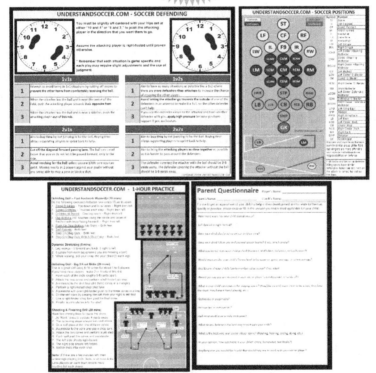

Go to this Link for an **Instant** Four-Page Printout:
UnderstandSoccer.com/free-printout

This FREE guide is simply a thank you for purchasing this book. This four-page printout will ensure that the knowledge you obtain from this book makes it to the field.

Table of Contents

Preface

Soccer Defending dives deep into how to position your body as a defender, when to be aggressive, and the keys to winning 1v1s, 2v1s, 1v2s, and 2v2s. Though the correct form and tactics are extremely helpful in ensuring the ball does not end up in your team's net, you also need a defender's mindset to improve on any weaknesses, solidify your strengths, and implement many techniques to become the person on your team that consistently dispossess the other team.

Soccer Positions reveals that each position requires players to develop different abilities and each position has its strengths and weaknesses. Understanding the position you want to play or the role you are already playing will make it easier to know exactly what to work on and learn.

Soccer Coaching discusses how average coaches only focus on the game-specific tactics. Great coaches know that working well with the parents, having the players trust you, and having strong game-specific tactics is a must. A great coach knows that there are hundreds of things that they can focus on but determining what 20% of things will produce 80% of the results is key to being as efficient of a coach as possible. **Therefore, *Soccer Coaching* is not meant to be a complete guide on coaching.** However, this book's main goal is to reveal the many key areas that can make a huge difference and are relatively easy to implement. This book gives you the techniques to become the coach that the parents want to work with, the soccer players love to play for, and the envy of all the other coaches in the league.

INDIVIDUAL SOCCER PLAYER'S PYRAMID

If you are looking to improve your skills, your child's confidence, or your players' abilities, then it is essential to understand where this book fits into the bigger picture of developing a soccer player. In the image, the most critical field-specific skills to work on are at the base of the Individual Soccer Player's Pyramid. Note: A team's pyramid may look slightly different based on the tactics the players can handle and the approach the coach decides to use for games. The pyramid is a quality outline to improve an individual soccer player's game. All the elements in the pyramid, and the items surrounding it, play a meaningful part in helping you become a better player, but certain skills should be read and mastered first before moving on to the others.

You will notice that passing and receiving is at the foundation of the pyramid. This is because if you can receive and make a pass in soccer, then you will be a useful teammate. Even though you may not consistently score, dispossess the other team, or dribble through several opponents, you will still have the fundamental tools needed to play the sport and contribute to your team.

As you move one layer up, you will find yourself with a decision to make on how to progress. Specifically, the pyramid is created with you in mind because each soccer player and each soccer position has different needs. Therefore, choose which path to take first based on the position you play—and more importantly, the position you *want* to play. In soccer and in life, just because you are in a particular spot, position, or job does not mean you have to stay there forever if that is not your choice. However, it is not recommended to refuse playing a position if you are not in the exact role you want yet. It takes time to develop the skills needed to shift from one position to another.

If you want to become a forward, then consider starting your route on the second layer of the pyramid with shooting and finishing. As your abilities to shoot increase, your coach will notice your new finishing skills and will be more likely to move you up the field (if you are not a forward already). Be sure to communicate to the coach that you desire to be moved up the field to a more offensive position, which will increase your chances, as well. If you are already a forward, then dive deep into this topic to ensure that you will become a leading scorer: first, on your team, and then in the entire league. Notice that shooting and finishing is considered to be less critical than passing and receiving. This is because you have to pass the ball up the field before you can take a shot on net.

Otherwise, you can start by progressing to dribbling and foot skills from passing and receiving because the proper technique is crucial to dribble the ball well. It is often necessary for a soccer player to use a skill to protect the ball from the other team or to advance the ball up the field, which will place their team in a favorable situation to score. The selection of this route is often taken first by midfielders and occasionally by forwards.

Defending is another option to proceed from passing and receiving. Keeping the other team off the scoreboard is not an easy task. Developing a defender's mindset, learning which way to push a forward, understanding how to position your body, knowing when to foul, and using the correct form for headers is critical for a defender on the back line who wants to prevent goals.

Finish all three areas in the second layer of the pyramid before progressing up the pyramid. Dribbling and defending the ball (not just shooting) are useful for an attacker; shooting and defending (not just dribbling) are helpful for a midfielder; while shooting and dribbling (not just defending) are helpful for a defender. Having a well-rounded knowledge of the skills needed for the different positions is important for all soccer players. It is especially essential for soccer players who will want to change positions in the future. Shooting and finishing, dribbling and foot skills, and defending are often more beneficial for soccer players to learn first, so focus on these before spending time on the upper areas of the pyramid. In addition, reading about each of these areas will help you understand what your opponent wants to do.

Once you have improved your skills in the first and second tiers of the pyramid, move up to fitness. It is difficult to go through a passing/dribbling/finishing drill for a few minutes without being out of breath. However, as you practice everything below the fitness category in the pyramid, your fitness and strength will naturally increase. Performing technical drills will allow soccer players to increase their fitness naturally. This reduces the need to focus exclusively on running for fitness.

Coming from the perspective of both a soccer player and trainer, I know that constantly focusing on running is not as fulfilling—nor does it create long-lasting improvements—whereas emphasizing shooting capabilities, foot skills, and defending knowledge will create long-lasting change. Often, coaches who focus on running their players in practice are also coaches who want to improve their team but have limited knowledge of the soccer-specific topics that would quickly increase their players' abilities. Not only does soccer fitness include your endurance; it also addresses your ability to run with agility and speed and to develop strength and power, while using stretching to improve your flexibility. All these tools put together leads to a well-rounded soccer player.

Similar to the tier below it, you should focus on the fitness areas that will help you specifically, while keeping all the topics in mind. For example, you may be a smaller soccer player who could use some size. In this case, you should emphasize weight training so that you can gain the muscle needed to avoid being pushed off the ball. However, you should still stretch before and after a lifting workout or soccer practice/game to ensure that you stay limber and flexible, which will help you recover quickly and avoid injuries.

Maybe you are a soccer player in your 20s, 30s, or 40s. In this case, emphasizing your flexibility would do a world of good to ensure that you will keep playing soccer for many more years. However, doing a few sets of push-ups, pull-ups, squats, lunges, sit-ups, etc. per week will also help you maintain or gain a desirable physique.

Furthermore, you could be in the prime of your career in high school, college, or at the pro level, which means that obtaining the speed and endurance needed to run for 90+ minutes is the most essential key to continue pursuing your soccer aspirations.

Finally, we travel to the top of the pyramid, which involves tryouts. Although tryouts occur only 1-2 times per year, they have a huge impact on whether you will make the team or get left out of the lineup. Tryouts can cause intense anxiety if you do not know the keys to make sure that you stand out from your competitors and are very confident from the start.

The last portion of the pyramid are the areas that surround it. Although these are not skills and topics that can be addressed by your physical abilities, they each play key roles in rounding out a complete soccer player. For example, having a supportive parent/guardian or two is beneficial, as they can help provide transportation to and from practices and games, the needed equipment, the fees for the team, the expenses for individual training, and most importantly, encouragement. Additionally, having a quality coach whose teachings and drills will help the individual learn how their performance and skills fit into the team's big picture will help a lot, too.

Obtaining enough sleep is critical to have enough energy during practices and on game days, as well as to recover from training and games. Additionally, appropriate soccer nutrition will increase a soccer player's energy and endurance, help them achieve the ideal physique, and significantly aid in their recovery.

Understanding soccer positions will help you determine if a specific role is well-suited for your skills. It is important to know there are additional types of specific positions, not just forwards, midfielders, and defenders. A former or current professional player in the same position can provide guidance on the requirements to effectively play that position.

Finally, you must develop a mindset that will leave you unshakable. This mindset will help you prepare for game situations, learn how to deal with other players, and become mentally tough enough to not worry about circumstances that you cannot control, such as the type of field you play on, the officiating, or the weather.

The pyramid is a great visual aid to consider when choosing which areas to focus on next as a soccer player, coach, or parent. However, remember that a team's pyramid may look slightly different, based on which tactics the players can handle and which approach the coach decides to use for games.

If you have not read the *Understand Soccer* series book, *Soccer Training*, then it is highly recommended that you do so to gain general knowledge of crucial topics within the areas of the pyramid. Picking up a copy of the book will act as a good gauge to see how much you know about each topic. This will additionally help determine if another *Understand Soccer* series book about a specific tier of the soccer pyramid will be beneficial for you.

Now that you know where this book plays into the bigger picture, let us begin. Remember that if there are any words or terms whose meaning you are unsure of; you can reference the glossary at the back of the book.

Finally, if you enjoy this book, please leave a review on Amazon to let me know.

Soccer Defending:

A Step-by-Step Guide on How to Stop the Other Team

Chapter 1

Focus on Your Primary Role

The game is on the line with only 30 seconds to go, and the score is tied. You, a defender, take a shot from the 30-yard line, and it is a fantastic upper-90 goal to win the game for your team. The fans cheer, your team celebrates your accomplishment, and you feel like you are on top of the world.

This story is just that—a story. It is great when it happens, but as a defender, it should not be how you judge your performance. What separates good defenders from great defenders is game intelligence. Therefore, let us review some high-level concepts that all defenders should understand:

1. Your biggest priority is to prevent goals.
2. Avoid dribbling in most circumstances.
3. Stay positive!
4. A small touch goes a long way.
5. Keep your hands wide when outside of your 18-yard box, and your hands behind you when inside of it.

1. **Your most significant objective as a defender is to keep the other team from scoring.** It is not to score or dazzle the fans with your foot skills but to prevent the other team from scoring. Therefore, it is okay to clear the ball up the field when

you are under extreme pressure inside your 18-yard box. It is okay for you to pass the ball off to the midfielders and forwards to let them do their jobs and provide the goals for your team. It is okay if you are not on the stat sheet for a goal or an assist.

2. **As a defender, you should mostly avoid dribbling the ball.** Look for passes and sometimes clearances. Soccer is a probability game, and if you lose the ball, then the forward on the other team will have fewer people to beat than they would have if the ball started at the opposition's defense. Remember, a defender is judged 90% by the number of goals scored against them and not by the flair of their dribbling abilities. However, you must also understand the defensive role on your team. The right-outside defender or left-outside defender may play as wingbacks, which means they are expected to dribble the ball up the field and cross it into the box.

3. **Do not forget about the things you are good at.** I get it; defending is tough! You are constantly throwing your body on the line for your team with minimal recognition. On most soccer teams, people often only notice defenders when they mess up, and the forwards are usually the ones who grab the glory. Accept that this is a reality and develop the mindset that it is most important to win as a team and not as an individual.

4. **Most times, all you need to do is slightly touch the ball.** Too many defenders feel that if they have not entirely

dispossessed the attacker and played the ball to a teammate, then they have not successfully performed their job. However, making contact—even with just a toe—will often mess up the attacking player's plan and prevent the ball from going into your net. As players on the other team attack against you, they will create plans to score. Therefore, just a simple and slight redirection of the ball while they are attempting to carry out their plan will often be more than enough to slow or completely stop the other team's forward progress.

5. **Allow your hands to be in a natural position outside your 18-yard box and keep them clasped behind you when you are inside your 18-yard box, and the other team has the ball.** Similar to the last point, a small touch on the ball will often stop an attacker's progress, as will a nudge with your arm. As a defender, it is crucial to play bigger than you are. The easiest way to do this is to keep your arms away from your body to make it more difficult for the attacking player to dribble around you. Additionally, this will make you appear bigger, which will in turn slightly reduce the attacker's confidence in their ability to dribble past you. If you are outside your 18-yard box, then having your arms up and your forearm against the attacker as they are receiving the ball is a phenomenal way to increase the difficulty of their first touch. Disrupting their first touch will help limit any additional moves after that if they cannot gain control of the ball.

Additionally, if the attacker is pushing the ball past you while they are dribbling, then do not be afraid to extend your arms in front of them to help prevent them from beating you to the ball. From a young age, soccer players are often taught that they must keep their hands perfectly by their sides. However, as you begin to play at higher levels, you will notice that most referees do not call players with their arms extended.

Play with a big presence—unless you are in your 18-yard box. Then, keeping your hands behind your body is important. If you are attempting to block a shot or cross, and the ball deflects off one of your arms, then you will give your opponent the easiest opportunity to score via a penalty kick.

When watching professional soccer games, you will often notice that just one minor mistake made by a defender in their own 18-yard box will often decide the outcome of a game. An accidental handball will allow the other team an uncontested shot on net from the penalty spot. This type of mental mistake is one of the easiest ways to destroy your team's momentum and lose your teammates' confidence in you.

Again, you must focus on your primary role which is to keep the ball out of your team's net. Many of the things we have briefly discussed here will be further expanded upon in the chapters to come. These concepts are great insights that every quality defender should implement into their game.

Chapter 2

Reading the Game and Playing Each Player Differently

Defenders are judged on many things. As mentioned in the first chapter, the most important thing for the entire defense is to prevent the other team from scoring. However, goals allowed do not make for the best measurement of a defender's effectiveness, since one mistake made by a defender other than yourself could result in a goal. Therefore, there are additional ways to track a defender's abilities by using the following metrics, listed in order of importance:

1. Recoveries
2. Interceptions
3. Blocks
4. Clearances

Recoveries are when a defender regains possession of the ball shortly after your team was dispossessed. **Recoveries are important because the best time to regain possession of the ball is within six seconds after it was stolen**, according to former player Pep Guardiola, who is one of the most successful coaches in the world. His methodology is to recover the ball with a six-second burst of high-intensity pressing. Often, the turnover occurs during the other team's half, so the press is performed by the forwards and midfielders. Having forwards and midfielders press the other team for the ball is known as "high-pressing" and doing it throughout the game will take considerable energy away from the forwards and midfielders who are responsible for scoring. This is why Guardiola tells his players to high-press for roughly six seconds, and then assume a standard defensive formation that takes less energy. All the players nearest the ball are required to rush towards the individual in possession, while the rest of the team will move closer together for a tighter defensive formation. The close players shut down passing options to force an immediate mistake. If no error occurs, then the tight positioning becomes the basis of a great defensive formation.

Reading the game is vital because intercepting a pass will display superior soccer intellect. It will show the defender's ability to anticipate, which is a critical aspect of becoming an intelligent soccer player. A defender who can anticipate will wait until the perfect time to step into a passing lane and intercept or deflect a pass.

Another important aspect of intercepting a pass is positioning. Being correctly positioned demonstrates an understanding of how a play develops in a game. Being in the right place at the right time will require familiarity with both your team's tactics and the other team's game plan.

For positioning, a good general rule of thumb is to stay between the attacking player and the goalie. Cutting off the attacker's angle to the net will make it easier to block shots. If an attacker gets past you on a wing, then typically the best way to recover is along a straight line between you and the near post. If the attacker strays out of that line, then hopefully it will take them near another defender on your team. If the defensive players on your team are beaten regularly, then you may want to switch to a formation in which most of the team is behind the ball. This is a strategy known as "parking the bus."

Next, remember that all players are different. While defending against attacking players on the opposing team, you must identify their strengths and weaknesses. It is essential to exploit their weaknesses and diminish the forwards' ability to use their strengths. This is how to do it:

1. Watch them in warm-ups/other games.
2. Communicate to your other defenders how you intend to defend the forward.
3. Change your plan, if needed.

Although it takes more time to scout the other team, it can pay off substantially. Without having seen a team or player before, you may make assumptions based on how they look, and this can be detrimental. If you make an assumption, then you may expect the taller players to be on the end of headers, all the team's opposing players to be right-footed, etc.

Let your teammates know how you intend to defend against attackers on the other team. Communicating this will allow you to hear their thoughts, too, and ensure that the entire back line is on the same page.

If you realize that your defensive plan is not working, then change the plan. Whether it is 15 minutes into the game or at halftime, change your plan to include what you have learned so far while playing against the other team.

Remember that each player on both teams has their own strengths and weaknesses. The more time you spend learning about the other team, communicating what you have learned, and developing a plan with your teammates; the easier it will be to keep the other team off the scoreboard. The hardest working players—both on and off the field—are often on their way to becoming the best soccer players, if they are not the best already.

Chapter 3

Body Positioning and the 1v1

As a defender, your body positioning should be angled. Never point your hips (i.e., "square") at the attacker completely because it will allow the attacker to go to the right of you, to the left of you, or between your legs. **You should be angled but not entirely turned to the side.** Position one of your sides so that it faces the attacker, but you are still at a diagonal. If your feet were hands on a clock, they would be positioned at either "10 and 4" (as shown in the first image) or "8 and 2" (as shown in the second image.)

This body positioning will allow you to push them either to the left or the right. Standing at "10 and 4" will push them to their left foot and standing at "8 and 2" will push them to their right foot. Keep in mind that just standing directly in front of them and turning your hips will not force them in the direction that you want them to go. **You must be slightly off-centered, with your hips set at either "10 and 4" or "8 and 2," to push them in the direction that you want them to go.**

If you just turn your hips directly in front of a good dribbler, then they will attack the side that you are not facing to make it easier to get around you. This will force you to turn farther to pursue them. Therefore, it is best to position yourself slightly closer to the side in which you do not want them to go. If they attack in the direction in which you are forcing them, then your positioning will make it easier for you to tackle or pursue.

As a defender, it is essential to stay active by being on your toes. You do not want to be caught standing still. You should remain in a low stance, bent at the knees and the hips. Being on your toes will allow you to accelerate faster when the attacker performs a skill and attempts to sprint away.

As discussed in the book, *Soccer Shooting & Finishing: A Step-by-Step Guide on How to Score*, great coaches and trainers will teach their soccer players the following three things while they are developing their 1v1 skills:

1. Use a foot skill.

2. Attack with speed.

3. Use your dominant foot to shoot.

A defender must understand what the other team's player is aiming to do with the ball in a 1v1. Learning their go-to tactics will allow you to develop a plan to stop them.

First, remember that the attacker often wants to use a foot skill. Using a foot skill such as a body feint or scissor may cause you, the defender, to turn your body in the wrong direction, thereby making it easier for the attacker to move past you. As a defender, you will need to address the situation even before the attacker obtains the ball. By applying significant pressure to them and stopping them from receiving a pass, you will not even need to worry about them performing a foot skill. However, if they receive the ball, then watch the direction of their hips when they perform the foot skill. Understand that a highly skilled attacker will misleadingly turn their hips in the direction that they want the defender to go. Luckily, most attackers are not experienced or knowledgeable enough and often show their true intentions with their hips.

Next, remember that the forward wants to attack with speed. This acceleration after a foot skill is critical for them to create the space and separation needed from the defender. As a result, you must look to interfere with their ability to accelerate. The best way to do this is to extend your arms to block the direction in which they want to go. Aim to slow them down or even nudge them as they are taking their next touch. This will force a mistake. Do not merely let them past you without doing everything in your power to prevent it!

Finally, whenever you defend in a 1v1 situation, remember that **one of the attacker's main goals is to take a shot with their dominant foot. Obviously, the foot they are more comfortable using will provide a more accurate and powerful shot, as compared to a shot with their opposite foot.** In a 1v1, a good striker will attempt to go in the direction they desire. However, a great defender will prevent them from going to their dominant foot. Therefore, not only is being at "10 and 4" or "8 and 2" important but standing slightly off-center to force the attacker to their opposite foot is necessary, too.

In a 1v1 game situation, the direction in which you will push the defender depends on the portion of the field they are on and their location relative to your teammates. Ideally, if you were in the middle of the field, then you should push the attacker to their weaker foot. How do you know which foot is their weaker foot? **Always assume it is their left foot until you observe otherwise.** However, along a sideline during a 1v1, you should position your body in a way that will push them out of bounds and towards the sideline. Notice in the following image that the defender is slightly to the attacker's right side, which will often force the attacker to their left.

At Next Level Training (NLT), the premier soccer training company in Michigan, we hired another trainer (who happens to have the same name as me!) Sure enough, a few months later, we ended up playing against each other in a league match. Keep in mind that this "other Dylan" is a great guy, and an excellent addition to our NLT staff. However, I was playing an attacking midfield position, and, at times, I had to defend against him.

As described previously, I followed the rule and forced him to his left foot when he had the ball. I soon found out that this was to his advantage, as he was left-footed. He struck a wonderful shot that barely missed the net, but I took a mental note of this for future use in the game. I ended up defending him several more times that game. Because I now knew that he was left-footed, I gave him more space to his right foot. This tactic worked well for the rest of the game, and he was unable to take another shot while I was defending him. Sadly, some of my teammates did not take my advice to push him to his opposite foot, and he ended up scoring two goals against us because they let him use his dominant foot.

In conclusion, your objectives when defending in a 1v1 are to: (1) prevent the defender from receiving the ball by applying pressure on them; (2) if they receive the ball, then watch out for a foot skill by focusing on their hips, while directing them to their opposite foot by using a slightly off-center stance;

and (3) if they successfully perform a foot skill, then use your arms by placing them in front of the attacker to slow their speed as they aim to accelerate past you.

Check out the *Understand Soccer* series book, *Soccer Dribbling & Foot Skills: A Step-by-Step Guide on How to Dribble Past the Other Team*, for various foot skills that trained attackers will use when attempting to dribble around you. Obtaining your opponent's knowledge will make it easier to learn how to stop them.

YouTube: If you would like to see a video on how to position your body as a defender, then consider watching the *Understand Soccer* YouTube video: *Body Positioning in Soccer*.

YouTube: If you would like to see a video on how to win a 1v1 while defending, then consider watching the *Understand Soccer* YouTube video: *Best 1v1 Defending*.

Chapter 4

Defending in a 2v1

When there is a 2v1, and you are the only defender against two attacking players, there are several helpful guidelines you can follow to increase your chances of preventing the other team from scoring or even shooting. They are as follows:

1. Aim to slow the speed of play as much as possible.
2. Block the diagonally-forward passing lane.
3. Use your effort to stopping the person with the ball.

When you are the only defender in a 2v1, your first priority should be to slow the play down as much as possible to allow teammates to sprint back and provide support. Since a 2v1 does not give you many options, your best bet to slow the speed of play is to keep considerable space (at least 5 yards) between you and the attackers while you are outside your 18-yard box. **Reducing the space between you and the attacking player who has possession of the ball will force the attacker to either: (1) perform a foot skill and sprint past you; or (2) pass the ball diagonally forward, so their teammate can run to the ball. Either of these options will speed up the play, which is exactly what you should avoid.** Considering that your primary aim is to keep the ball out of your net, you do not necessarily need to regain possession of the ball yourself if you can buy time for a teammate to do it with more favorable odds. Remember that the defensive objective of preventing the other team from scoring is more important than receiving glory for a spectacular play.

Being the only defender in a 2v1 places you at a huge disadvantage, and you must decide whether to shut down the person with the ball or cut off the passing lane. Understand that this is very situational, and each 2v1 will look slightly different. In general, you should aim to shut down the player with the ball, while blocking the diagonally-forward passing lane. **A horizontal pass on the field from one striker to the other is excellent for the defender because the ball will not advance up the field with this pass, which will provide an additional second or two for your supporting teammates to travel back towards the play.**

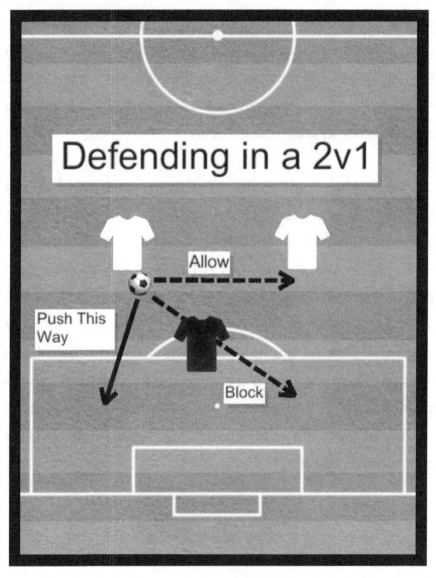

Next, your primary focus should be on the person with the ball. Push them towards the end line; this will decrease their angle towards the net if they decide to shoot. Notice that in the above image, the defender is not directly in front of the attacker but is cutting off the diagonally-forward passing lane and giving the defender some space to attack along the sideline without using their teammates' help. **In essence, your goal should be**

to turn the 2v1 into a 1v1 by positioning yourself to take the other attacker out of the play.

The worst thing you can do in this situation is reach for the ball, miss it, and allow an easy breakaway for two players on the other team. This will nearly always end up in the back of the net because the goalie must then position themselves to stop the person with the ball. However, a simple pass to the other player will leave the entire net wide-open for an easy tap-in goal.

In conclusion, you should first aim to slow the speed of play, then cut off the diagonally-forward passing lane and place the majority of your focus on the attacker with the ball. Work to turn the 2v1 into a 1v1, while providing time for your teammates to travel back into position. Avoid reaching/lunging for the ball, unless you know with 100% certainty that you will dispossess the attacker; otherwise, you will risk the terrible situation of a two-person breakaway.

YouTube: If you would like to see a video on how to win a 2v1 while defending, then consider watching the *Understand Soccer* YouTube video: *How to Defend 2v1 in Soccer*.

Chapter 5

Defending in a 1v2

When you are one of two defenders who are taking on a single attacker, it is critical to make it as easy as possible to prevent the attacker from scoring. To do this, you must ask yourself, "How can I best stop the attacker and regain possession of the ball to start a counterattack?"

A good striker will travel slightly to the outside, where they only need to beat one defender to shoot the ball. Conversely, a good defender will force the attacker into their supporting teammate. All it takes to do this is correct positioning in relation to the attacker. You should not position yourself directly in front of the attacker but slightly off to the side, so the attacker has an easier route past you on one side. However, that should be the side where your supporting defender is. See the following image for an example:

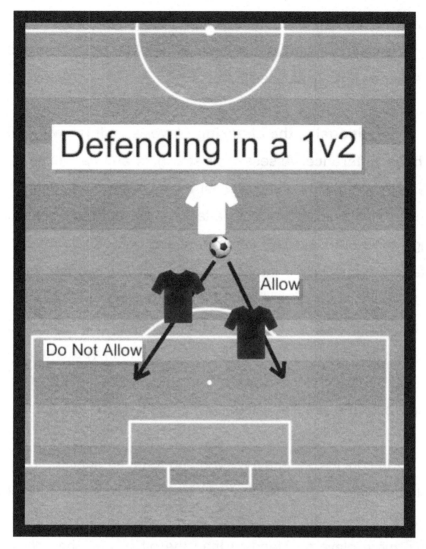

Notice that the first defender is forcing the attacker toward their teammate. This is good advice for a 1v3, when you are defending an attacker with two additional teammates. **The overarching goal is for your team to have a more favorable advantage when you are defending. The 1v2 provides this advantage over a 1v1.** Aim to force the attacking player to take on all the defenders before they can shoot. In these instances, when you have more players, you should not wait for the attacker's teammates to come support the player. Therefore, be aggressive and speed up the pace of the play to dispossess the attacker as quickly as possible.

Additionally, the attacking player's abilities will make a huge difference. Assess their strengths and determine how closely you should defend against them. When more defenders are working against the sole attacking player, you should be aggressive but leave 2-3 yards of space between you and the attacker—especially if they are a great dribbler. Giving a bit of space will make it more difficult for the attacker to use a foot skill to accelerate past you and the other defender. However, if the attacker's strength is their shooting ability, then you should not be any farther than 1-2 yards from them. You should aim to dispossess the attacker without giving them space to shoot.

In conclusion, in a 1v2, you can force an attacker to beat both defenders by positioning your body so that they are pushed towards your teammate. Speed up the pace of play while you have more players defending than the other team has players attacking to avoid giving additional opposing attackers enough time to support their teammate. Furthermore, assess the attacker's foot skills and shooting ability. Provide a yard or two more of space if they are a better dribbler than shooter.

YouTube: To see a video on how to win a 1v2 while defending, then watch the *Understand Soccer* YouTube video: *2v1 Defending*.

Chapter 6

Defending in a 2v2

A 2v2 is a typical scenario that defenders will find themselves in during a game. Clearly, the best way to defend is to avoid unfavorable situations altogether. Cutting off passing lanes, being in the correct position, and having several players behind the ball (i.e., between the ball and their own net) will reduce the need to recover from a situation in a game in which only a few players are involved.

However, since this does not always happen, this chapter will teach you how to prevent the other team from scoring a goal during a 2v2 when you are in the defending third of the field. Consider the following things to increase your chances of successfully stopping the two attacking players:

1. Slow the forwards' momentum to allow your teammates to hustle back.
2. Bring both the attackers as close together as possible.
3. Focus on positioning based on which attacker has the ball.

Even if you and your defending teammate do not steal the ball immediately, you both will be considered successful if you can slow the attackers' progress up the field enough for your teammates to come back into position

and help defend. Stalling the attacking player's momentum in 1v1s, 2v1s, and 2v2s will make it much easier to defend. Limiting their forward progress will increase the chance that your supporting teammates can hustle back into position to become additional defenders, and it will reduce the chance that the attacking players will sprint past you. Again, placing your arms in the way of the attacking player, making yourself bigger by keeping your arms spread, and maintaining a moderately wide stance will go a long way to slow the attackers' progress. In addition, if you are covering the attacking player, then keeping 2-3 yards of space between you and the defender with the ball will provide enough space to limit the effectiveness of the attacking player's foot skill, thereby crushing their chance for an explosive push of the ball. Furthermore, this will not allow the attacking player to create space between you and them.

Avoid allowing the forwards to create several yards of space between you and your teammate. Allowing too much space between you and your teammate will give the attacking player with the ball more options, and thus a greater chance to score. Specifically, if they elect not to pass the ball but to dribble their defender instead, then they will not have to beat the additional defender, as well. Furthermore, if the attacking player with the ball decides to pass the ball, then allowing the other attacking player to be farther from their teammate will increase the chance of creating an open lane behind the defender. Keep in mind that a 2v2 is very situational.

A 2v2 in your own third of the field will differ greatly from a 2v2 when your opponent is not within striking distance.

If you and your teammate can move the two attackers closer together, then there is an increased chance for you and your teammate to dispossess the attackers. Four feet swinging at the ball and trying to poke it away, instead of just two, will double your chance of success. To avoid being too close together, attackers will often run into space, hoping to enable an easy pass from their teammate. **Often, a great attacking player will take their first 2-3 steps in the wrong direction,** hoping you will begin to cut them off, which will provide them with enough space to run in the direction they actually want to go.

In the league match against the "other Dylan" of Next Level Training, mentioned previously in this book, there was one instance when I was defending against him about 20 yards away from the net. His teammate on the opposite wing had the ball, and I was following the rule of forcing him to his opposite foot (which, if you recall from earlier in the book, was his right foot). However, to my surprise, after his initial two steps towards his dominant foot, he quickly cut and exploded towards his right (and towards the ball!) Unfortunately, this misleading run provided him with enough space to travel a step or two past me. The worst part about this was that he was now at the penalty spot, while I was sprinting to recover. Luckily, the "other Dylan's" teammate attempted a pass to him that was blocked. Had it not been; his misleading run would have produced an easy shot on net because while he did not have possession of the ball, I did not stay 3-5 yards away while defending against him. I was only about two yards away from him when he used his very misleading run. Keeping 3-5 yards of space between you and the attacker without the ball will decrease their chance of making make a quality run past you, and thus they will be less likely to be passed the ball by their teammate.

Understand that if you are covering the attacker without the ball in a 2v2, then you must be closer to the net than your teammate who is covering the attacking player with the ball. There are two reasons to be positioned this way. First, if the ball is passed, then you will have time to adjust your position and move closer to the player to whom the ball was passed. However, if you are guarding the player without the ball, and you are farther from the net than your teammate, then you will allow the player with the ball an easy passing lane to take advantage of, which will almost guarantee them a shot on goal.

The other reason to position yourself closer to the net than your teammate is that if the opponent whom your teammate is guarding dribbles past your teammate with the ball, then you will be positioned properly to run over and provide help.

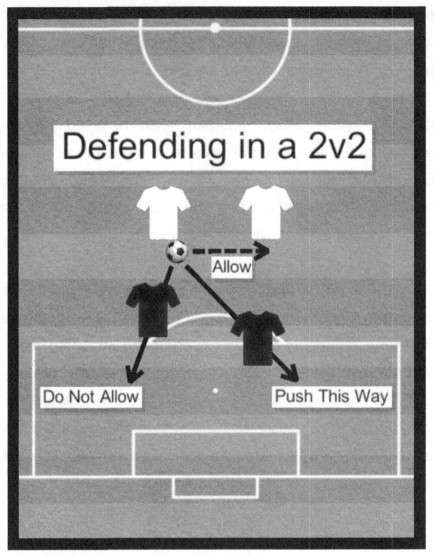

Notice in the image above that the defender closest to the player with the ball is 2-3 yards away. However, the defender who is covering the attacker without the ball is 3-5 yards from that player. If the ball were to be played horizontally to the other attacker, then the ball would not make any progress up the field, and it would give your other teammates enough time to hustle back to support. **If this were to happen, then the**

defender who is covering the person who just passed the ball would drop back so that they were 3-5 yards from the player without the ball. The other defender would then minimize the space between themselves and the attacker who received the ball to only 2-3 yards. In essence, the right defender in the image would shift forward if the ball were played to the attacker whom they were defending, and the left defender would shift backward to put more space between the attacking player and themselves.

Finally, a key point to remember is to be explosive in these types of situations to avoid allowing the attacking players to catch you and your teammate flat-footed. By keeping pace with the player whom you are covering, you will increase the chance of your team preventing a goal. Therefore, be active and on your toes. Constantly talk to your teammate and tell them if you need them to adjust something and communicate your intentions as the play unfolds.

If you are looking for drills with specific coaching points to use in practices that will increase your player's skills, then grab a copy of the *Understand Soccer* series book, *Soccer Drills*.

YouTube: If you would like to see a video on how to win a 2v2 while defending, then consider watching the *Understand Soccer* YouTube video: *Soccer 2v2*.

Chapter 7

Reading the Attacking Player's Foot Skills

Understand that a well-executed move does not have any tells that will make it easy for you to know what the person with the ball will do. Sometimes, you will simply be beaten by an effective skill. However, reading the other player's body language will help ensure that these situations are few and far between.

Reading an attacker's foot skill implies that you are waiting for the attacker to act so that you may *react*. **A defender who aims to react is one who prefers to block shots, wait for the attacker to make a mistake, and dispossess an attacker before they can perform a foot skill.** The other type of defender is one who prefers to prevent the attacker from receiving the ball and is continually reaching in to steal possession of the ball or at least poke it away. You will need to recognize the following foot skills to help stop an attacking player:

1. Shot Fake
2. Body Feint or Scissor
3. Self-Pass or Roll

To determine whether an attacking player is faking a shot or taking a shot, you must consider a few things. **For an actual shot, a player's arms go up, their leg contracts far behind their body, and they will likely look at the net before they shoot** (although not all players who strike the ball will look at the net before shooting.) Study the attacker's shooting form during warm-ups to recognize their shooting style. Yes, this will take extra time beforehand, but it can save you from not knowing how to defend against the attacker at the start of a game.

Knowing when the attacker is performing a scissor or body feint is necessary for the reactive defender. In a poorly executed body feint or scissor, the ball will often start directly in front of the attacker, rather than slightly diagonal to one side or the other, which is how it should correctly begin. **More importantly, in a successful body feint or scissor, the attacker should turn their shoulders and hips toward the direction in which they want you to think they are going. However, in a poorly executed body feint or scissor, the attacker will not do this.** Therefore, the attacker's legs may show that they are faking one way, but their upper body will tell you a different story. Additionally, **most players' legs will not travel all the way back when they fake a shot.** They will bend at the knee but will not bend at the hip. They can still generate some power by using a windup like this, but most shots will involve a full windup and not just a modest bend at the knee.

For a self-pass or roll, you cannot read into the attacker's actions because these skills are performed only after you have overcommitted and lunged for the ball. These skills are the attacker's *reaction* to the defender's *action.* **Therefore, lunging for the ball is not often recommended—unless you are 100% certain that you will dispossess the attacker, or you have many players behind you to recover if you miss, and the attacker speeds past you.**

In conclusion, look for differences between a shot fake and a shot. An attacker's body will often point in the direction they intend to travel. Some defenders will bait the attacker by intentionally faking out the defender(e.g., leaving a lane open for the attacker to dribble or pass the ball) but closing it down at the last second. In each situation, you must determine whether it is better to be the first defender to act or to react based on the attacker's moves.

Chapter 8

Being Physical and Knowing When to Foul

As previously mentioned, one of the best ways to be physical is to extend your arms in front of the attacking player to slow them down. From a young age, players are taught to keep their arms by their sides. However, **in a game, the referee will hardly ever call a foul on you if your arms are against an opponent.** If the referee is not usually going to make a call when your arms are against an opponent, then use this to your advantage.

The trick here is to not grab them or put your hands on them. **Extend your elbow and shoulder to engage with them.** It is crucial that you make yourself look bigger because this will make it harder for the opposing player to travel around you. Keeping your arms up will make it easier for you to place your forearm against their body and use your shoulder muscle to keep them away from the ball. When you watch professional defenders, you will notice that they tend to use their hands and arms a lot. This is because in most situations, the referee will not call anything against them.

As a defender, you will often find yourself being the only player left between the attacker and an easy shot on your goalkeeper. Therefore, it is essential to know when to lunge for the ball, and when to continue to backpedal so that your teammates can sprint back and help stop the attacker. As a rule of thumb, if it is a 1v1 situation with just you standing between the attacker and the goal, then you should backpedal to wait for the opportunity to block their shot, while also attempting to push them towards their weak foot by using your body positioning. Unless you are 100% sure that you will succeed in kicking the ball away or taking possession of it, you should avoid lunging for the ball. **This is key because if you miss the ball, the attacker will quickly dribble around you, and they will have a breakaway against the keeper.**

When jockeying (i.e., backpedaling while keeping the defender in front of you), your momentum will be going in the same direction as the attacker. Both bodies are moving towards your own goal. **However, reaching for the ball will change your body's momentum from going backward to going forward.** Changing your momentum is significant because if you miss the ball, then you will need to come to a complete stop and quickly accelerate into a sprint and recover from your mistake. This rarely happens; instead, the attacker will often take an easy shot during their breakaway. Therefore, in 1v1 situations, you should react based on the attacker's move. If they attempt to shoot the ball, then make sure you block it. If they attempt to dribble, then force them to their weaker foot and push them towards the sideline to decrease the angle with which they can approach the net.

However, when more teammates are alongside and behind you, it is appropriate to reach for the ball because even if you miss, your teammates will support you and help cover for your mistake. In this case, lunging with the intention to steal the ball is an acceptable risk that can start a counterattack, while the other team's defense has not yet established their shape to defend properly. Remember that this is only a general rule, and specific situations will differ. Therefore, develop both your skills and ability to judge the situation.

In soccer, there are certain instances when it is acceptable to foul (although it is never advisable to tell someone to hurt an opposing player intentionally.) **A tactical foul is appropriate when your team is slow to defend, and there are more attackers than defenders behind the ball.** In this instance, a tactical foul to stop the play may be appropriate. Although yellow cards are not fun to obtain, remember that they are just a warning. Simply holding a player or extending your leg too far out while the attacker is dribbling can create the time needed for your team to position more players between the ball and the net because of the foul you committed that the referee called.

In conclusion, use your arms to slow your opponent down and consider making a necessary tactical foul. Avoid lunging for the ball when you do not have teammates to help but be sure to attempt to steal the ball when you have plenty of supporting teammates behind you. Be physical and use your judgment while defending to determine what works best for you in each situation. Understand that there is a right time to commit to stealing the ball, and a right time to wait for the attacker to act first. The better the attacker is; the more you should respect their foot skills and position yourself to avoid being out-skilled by them. Vincent Kompany and Pepe are great examples of defenders who are very physical and use their aggressiveness to their advantage.

YouTube: If you would like to see a video on how to be physical and to know when to foul, then consider watching the *Understand Soccer* YouTube video: _Being Physical in Soccer & How to Foul in Soccer_.

Chapter 9

Slide Tackling

Disclaimer: Slide tackling may or may not be allowed in your league. Certain younger and non-competitive leagues often have rules against slide tackling. Therefore, make sure you are allowed to slide tackle before implementing any of the recommendations in this chapter.

First, consider a quote by Paolo Maldini, a left back and central defender for A.C. Milan and the Italian national team. Maldini is regarded as one of the best defenders of all time. However, he only averaged one tackle every two games. **In his words, *"If I have to make a tackle, then I have already made a mistake."***

Even Xabi Alonso, the former Liverpool, Real Madrid, and Bayern Munich holding midfielder, once stated, *"I don't think tackling is a quality. It is something you have to resort to, not a characteristic of your game."* Alonso makes an excellent point: Slide tackling should be a last-resort tactic.

Slide tackling is usually the result of a soccer player who was caught out of place and wants to make a last-ditch effort to recover the ball. **Slide tackling causes wear-and-tear on your body and can cause injury to the other player, too—**

which should always be avoided. Do not be a player who intends to hurt others. Just look at Sergio Ramos, who caused the entire nation of Egypt and the Liverpool fanbase to dislike him because of his aggressive tackle against Mohamed Salah a few weeks before the 2018 World Cup. Although this was not a slide tackle, Ramos still caused a shoulder injury to Liverpool's EPL record holder of 32 goals, who was forced to leave the UEFA Champions League Final before halftime and not return to the game.

If you aim to make slide tackling a part of your defensive game, then wearing the appropriate gear will help tremendously. **Soccer sliders are basically underpants with padding to prevent your legs from being torn up while sliding.** If you slide on turf or inadequate grass fields, then you will probably create a "strawberry" on your thigh. A strawberry (also known as a "raspberry" or "road rash") is a friction burn on the skin of your hip/upper leg caused by slide tackling. Turf fields are the biggest culprits for strawberries, and soccer sliders can help prevent these. Although sliders are helpful on grass fields, they are not as necessary. However, they can still help reduce physical injuries caused by slide tackling.

Next, only commit to slide tackling when you are 100% certain that you will touch the ball before making contact with the other player. It will almost certainly be a yellow card or a red card if your slide tackle is from behind and prevents the other team from scoring. Therefore, when you slide tackle, aim to either trap the ball between your toes and shin, so you can quickly attack in the other direction or strike it with the bone of your foot (where the leather meets the laces) to boot the ball (either to a teammate or out of bounds). During a slide tackle, you are committing to going to the ground, which will take some time to stand up and travel back into position from. Therefore, if you slide tackle, and the ball still rolls to the other team, then you will surely be caught out of position.

Lastly, when performing a slide tackle, it is key to travel fast enough to slide across the grass effectively. **Therefore, slide tackling requires running at full speed and sliding foot-first to either dispossess the other team or block their**

shot. Jogging and then attempting to slide tackle will most likely not get the job done.

In summary, remember that slide tackling should be used as a last resort and should be avoided in most situations. Make sure to use sliders under your shorts to prevent physical injuries. Slide only when you are 100% sure that you will touch the ball first. Finally, be sure to run fast enough to make your slide tackle as effective as possible.

Chapter 10

How to Shield the Ball

This chapter is an excerpt from the *Understand Soccer* series book, *Soccer Passing & Receiving*. It is crucial to protect the ball to ensure that you can distribute it to your teammates. To shield the ball appropriately as a defender, you must consider the following three things:

1. Maintain a low center of gravity.
2. Spread your arms.
3. Push the ball away from pressure.

When shielding the ball with an opposing player behind you, **it is vital to maintain a lower center of gravity than the**

opponent who is reaching for the ball. A lower center of gravity will give you a solid foundation, which will make it nearly impossible for the other player to move you and take possession of the ball.

Your center of gravity is how high your hips are from the ground. So, within reason, bringing your hips down several inches will make you more stable and harder to push off the ball. This positioning is similar to that of a quarter squat, wherein you squat one-quarter of the way down. This position is optimal to shield the ball from the other team.

Keep your arms out. Keeping your arms out means extending both at the shoulder and the elbow to make your body and your arms as wide as possible. The referees will hardly ever call you for keeping your arm raised—especially when you are shielding the ball from a player on the other team. Keeping your arms out and using them as leverage to make it harder for the opposition to steal the ball will also increase your chance of effectively shielding the ball and passing it to a teammate. In addition, keeping your arms out will naturally make your stance wider, and therefore it will take longer for the opposing player to travel around your body to steal the ball. Even if the opponent does manage to get around you, you can take a touch away from them to buy you more time. Use the area on your forearm between your wrist and elbow to make contact and provide the best advantage while giving enough space between the ball and the defender.

When shielding a ball, it is important not to be afraid to take a touch away from pressure. **A touch away from pressure will help generate some momentum and buy you more time to decide how you will pass the ball to a teammate.** If a player on the other team is coming to your right side from behind you, then push the ball towards the left, and vice versa. Keeping the ball on the side that is away from the opposition will allow you to keep your entire body between the ball and the opposing player.

Obviously, your size and the size of your opponent will make a difference. If you are a 5'5" soccer player, and you are going up against a 6'5" opponent, then you will find their leg length and natural strength will make it difficult for you to shield the ball. **If you are at a significant size disadvantage, then you should avoid situations in which you may be required to shield the ball.**

In conclusion, keep your center of gravity low by going a quarter of the way down into a squat. Spread your arms out at the shoulder and elbow, so they are wide and away from you. Do not be afraid to move the ball away from pressure temporarily to ensure that you can shield the ball properly.

For a great example of a small player who follows the concepts in this chapter to shield the ball effectively from his opponents, watch Philipp Lahm, the German National Team star and Bayern Munich player.

YouTube: If you would like to see a video on how to shield the ball, then consider watching the *Understand Soccer* YouTube video: *How to Shield the Ball*.

Chapter 11

Shot Blocking and Recovering After a Foot Skill

As a defender, shot blocking is a useful skill that allows you to frustrate the attacking players and dramatically change the speed and direction of a shot. You can apply the skills you learned in the Chapter on *Reading the Other Player's Foot Skills* to maintain great positioning and increase your ability to block shots when the attacking player attempts to create space and shoot the ball. **However, when there is space between you and the attacker, you must prioritize blocking certain shots.**

Obviously, you will want to block every shot, but you must first **emphasize stopping the shots that will be difficult for your goalkeeper to save**. At higher levels, goalkeepers become increasingly difficult to beat. Shots that are powerful or well-placed are likely the only ones that will give the shooter a chance to score. Therefore, when you are a few yards from the defender, and you want to block their shot, know that your main priority is to block the shooting lane that will be hardest for your goalkeeper to save.

When you watch some defenders block shots, you will notice they position themselves directly between the goalie and the ball. This is deficient for two reasons: **(1) it will be difficult** for the goalie to see the ball and react quickly enough to make a save if you cannot block the shot.; and (2) shots aimed directly at the goalkeeper will nearly always be saved by the goalkeeper.

Now, imagine the attacking player is striking the ball from the 18-yard box. Ideally, you should get close enough to block all shots, but your priority should be to prevent the ball from traveling to the far post (i.e., the spot in the net farthest from the goalkeeper.) Shots to the far post are what a goalkeeper is worried about, not shots that are close to their body. **Think about it: When you are standing directly between the ball and the goalkeeper, you are a couple of yards away from the ball, and so you are preventing a shot from going towards a portion of the net that your goalie is also covering.** Your team now has two players covering the same portion of the net, but they are still allowing a bent/curved shot to find its way around them both to the uncovered far post. Therefore, you should set up in front of the attacker to cut off any shots to the far post that they take from their preferred foot.

When you want to block the shot, consider lowering one knee to the ground to prevent the shooter from nutmegging you. This will also allow you to protect a wider area and prevent most shots on the ground by keeping your leg low and parallel to the ground.

Sadly, there will be times when you are defeated by an attacking player's foot skill. Another essential part of being a good defender is recovering after being dribbled past. Although it can be frustrating to know you messed up, you must take actions to recover.

Often, other defenders will help cover and buy time for the beaten defender to regain the correct positioning. However, you will not always have help, and you may have to recover on your own to avoid an easy breakaway for the other team. Clearly, speed plays a significant part, and superior speed will allow a defender to catch up to the person dribbling the ball and use their body/shoulder to push them off the ball or limit their shot.

Even if it does not seem like you will catch up, you must never forfeit the play. There have been countless times when a defender mentally forfeited the play, only to see the attacking player make a mistake with their next touch, or to see the goalkeeper make an excellent save but give up a rebound. In most instances, these rebounds could have been easily cleared if the defender had recovered correctly. Therefore, even if you are beaten, you should still begin running at full speed towards the nearest goalpost.

To beat you, it is likely that the attacking player will have to use a skill that requires them to change their direction, which means they will no longer be attacking directly towards the net. This change in direction takes time and may provide you with an opportunity to recover from your mistake. **Sprinting towards the nearest post will create the shortest distance for you to recover and increase your chance to block a shot. However, keep in mind that each situation is different and use your best judgment accordingly.**

The defender often has less space to cover than the opposing player and can travel to cut off the angles for a shot— even if they cannot dispossess the attacker. **Most soccer players cannot time their shot correctly during a full sprint.** This will give you additional time, as they will have to slow a bit to strike the ball. Do not forget that just your presence may cause fear in the attacking player, thereby forcing them to make a poor decision, a mistake, or to rush their shot. Defenders must always sprint to recover and can only stop once their team has regained possession of the ball, or the other team has scored.

To summarize, you should aim to block every shot but make sure to primarily block the shots that the goalkeeper will have a tough time saving. Furthermore, be sure to never give up—even if the attacker has beaten you. You have never been entirely beaten unless the ball is in the back of the net! Even if you do make a mistake, and your team is scored on, keep your head held high because it takes multiple mistakes by several players on your team for a goal to be scored. Also, it takes many mistakes by each player over the course of an entire game for your team to lose. So, wipe the momentary defeat out of your mind and continue to play as hard as you can!

Chapter 12

Heading the Ball

Heading the ball is a skill that should be mastered by all soccer players but is especially vital for defenders who want to prevent the other team from scoring. Since this book focuses on defending, this chapter will emphasize heading the ball to stop the other team from scoring.

First, when performing a header in soccer, it is essential to contract your body and neck forward by pulling your arms backward. **Contracting your body and neck will allow you to snap your body forward and accelerate your head quickly towards the ball, which will dramatically increase the power of your header.** Make sure to head through the ball to ensure even more power and more accuracy. This portion of heading is easily learned but judging the flight of the ball to time your jump appropriately will take practice and experience.

Shorter players, like Lionel Messi, who is 5'7", do not attempt many headers, due to their stature; instead, they look for defenders to misjudge a header, which gives them an easy scoring opportunity. However, whether you are a 5'5" defender or a 6'5" defender, you should practice your ability to clear the ball using your head. **When doing a header, use your forehead, _not_ the top of your head, for more accuracy.** However, to deflect the ball when it is being crossed, it is appropriate to use the top of your head if you cannot make contact with the ball using your forehead. It is tough to be accurate when the top of your head is used because your eyes will be off the ball for a significant amount of time. To ensure accuracy on your headers, you must keep your eyes open until a split-second before the ball hits your head.

Now, let us discuss one of the most important times in a game that you will need to head the ball—a corner kick. The two most common defensive tactics during a corner kick are: (1) man-marking players, and (2) having each defender and midfielder cover a zone. Whether you are man-marking or covering a zone, looking at where the opposing players are located will allow you to know in which direction you should clear the ball.

When a forward is attempting a header, and they are farther away than the penalty spot, avoid contact with them, as it is very unlikely that their header will have enough power to travel past a goalkeeper. However, if the forward is in the six-yard box, then make sure you make contact with the forward to disrupt their header (if you cannot head the ball away yourself).

During a corner kick, forwards are constantly moving to evade you. Often, forwards will recruit other teammates to set picks and obstruct your path. Therefore, make sure to communicate when you need help. Also, keep your head on a swivel by constantly checking over your shoulders to ensure that you are aware of any forwards in your blind spot. Having to choose between keeping your eyes on the ball or looking at the attacker is not a situation you want to be in as a defender.

Conversely, when your team is attacking and is on the other team's half, heading the ball is important to ensure that you can push the ball up the field and continue your team's attack. One way to overwhelm another team is to head any clearances back towards their net, which will allow you to continually attack. To do this effectively, you must be 100% certain that you can head the ball back into play. **Avoid going for the header if you are the last player on the back line of your team.** Forwards who know they are unlikely to win a header will hope it will go over your head, so they will have easy access to the net with the ball.

In summary, be sure to contract your whole upper body, not just your neck, to hit the ball harder with your head. Too many soccer players—myself included, at times—will allow the ball to hit them in the head, causing the ball to deflect softly towards the net or be passed to a teammate. **Not extending at the neck will create weak headers, which can be easily fixed by using your entire body to create a much more powerful header.** Additionally, be more physical with the other team's players the farther they are away from the net.

YouTube: If you would like to see a video on how to head the ball as a defender, then consider watching the *Understand Soccer* YouTube video: *How to Win Headers as a Defender*.

Chapter 13

Defending Against Fast Restarts

Restarts happen when the ball has gone out of bounds or has been awarded to a team because of a foul. The ball must be sent back into play for the game to continue. Restarts are a perfect opportunity for your opponent to catch your team off-guard. More than likely, your team will take a few seconds to travel into the correct positions, so they can defend the ball when it comes back into play. Frequently, defending teams will not hustle hard enough to get into position during a restart. They may need to catch their breath or take a few seconds for a mental break. **If the other team quickly places the ball back into play for a "fast restart," then it can create a quick disadvantage for your team.**

As an example, I use fast restarts to my advantage when playing offense during a corner kick. I will run as fast as I can to grab the ball, place it on the quarter circle, near the flag, and then immediately look for a teammate who is making a delayed run into the box or is open and checking to the corner flag. A quick corner kick is useful because the defense is likely not set up optimally enough to defend, and many defenders will not look at the ball when you first kick it into the 18-yard box. Before the start of the game, I communicate what I intend to do when I am restarting the ball to my teammates, so they will know to set up quickly for me to pass the ball to them.

However, this can be easily overcome by the other team if a defender or the goalkeeper immediately starts barking out orders. This ensures that everyone on the defending team is in position to defend the corner kick—no matter how quickly it is played into the box. This is incredibly demotivating; it can halt your team's momentum and often results in finger-pointing when the other team scores what you may consider a "cheap" goal because your team was not paying attention.

Although the team that is scored on may view it as a "cheap goal," it is great when your team is the one scoring because, simply put, *a goal is a goal.* When a quick goal is scored against your team from a fast restart, it is mentally challenging to overcome. Communication builds chemistry. So, be sure to establish before a game that there should be no mental breaks if your team is caught off-guard during a restart. Also, consider having a player stand directly in front of the ball on set pieces to buy a few more seconds of time for your team to become organized.

As stated in the *Understand Soccer* series book, *Soccer Passing & Receiving*, always make sure to **yell, don't call, and demand, don't ask**. If you are the leader in the backfield, then yell your orders with confidence. Demand that the players go to their correct positions; do not ask them to do it. Shouting with conviction will ensure that your teammates follow your orders immediately. Defenders and the goalkeeper have the best view of the field, and where everyone is positioned. So, be a leader by directing people to where they will be most effective.

Additionally, remember that since the other team is attempting to catch you off-guard, you should be sure to return the favor. Turn their fast restart into a counterattack for your team since many of the opposing players likely will have pushed up the field to support the restart. **When clearing the ball, either have a predetermined spot up one wing, where a forward will be located, or clear it in the space just past the opposing team's defensive line.** The area just beyond the opposing team's defensive line is very dangerous for them. A forward can run into this space to receive the ball and force the defenders to turn their backs on the direction in which they need to score. Do not clear the ball to the area in front of the defenders on the other team because they will just kick or head the ball back to begin another attack.

In conclusion, to defend against fast restarts, do not take a mental or physical break, and immediately yell out orders. Finally, make sure to clear the ball to either a predetermined spot or behind the other team's defensive line to start a fast break.

Chapter 14

Clock Management

Soccer is a sport with a fixed amount of time. Unlike baseball, tennis, and golf, soccer is both a competition against the other team and a race against the clock. Due to the set amount of time, managing the clock is essential. Often, games will have a scoreboard clock, so all players, coaches, and spectators will know precisely how much time is remaining. **If there is no scoreboard clock, then a coach or two on your team should use their own watch to ensure that they are correctly managing the remaining time.** Let us discuss a few ways to control the clock and use it as an additional way to prevent goals by the other team.

You should first consider your team's style of play, and the tactics that the coach chooses. However, one of the worst things a team can do is to go purely into a defensive mode if they score an early goal. The goal has just generated momentum for your team and switching to a defensive mindset will limit your team's ability to provide a cushion of two or three more goals. However, if your team has a great forward, and a solid defense, then you should absolutely look for opportunities to counterattack but also avoid limiting your team's play style too early in the game. The longer you focus on defense early in a game; the more relaxed you will become. This will increase the chance of the opposing team closing the passing lanes and eventually intercepting a pass in a position to create a quick counterattack. Therefore, playing too defensively is a risk you should avoid taking.

I have a good friend and teammate named Toni Sinistaj, who is always very ungenerous with restarts on the soccer field when his team is ahead. He does whatever he can to buy his team more time by taking longer to give the ball to the other team or making sure that his team is in the position they need to be before giving the ball to the person who is taking the throw-in. **He does a great job avoiding placing his team in a disadvantaged position when he has the power to do something about it.**

I always give him a hard time for using this tactic anytime I am on the other team in a practice, scrimmage, or pick-up game because I am trying to help my team win. However, I respect him and his strategy because it helps his team and is entirely within the rules. **However, if you are going to implement this strategy, then avoid taking too long to do it because you will receive a yellow card from the referee for delaying the game.** This seemingly petty tactic might not be received well by the other team. But remember that you are playing a competitive sport and using clock management strategies can be the difference between winning and losing a game.

During the game, by promptly giving the other team the ball, you are letting them win a small battle. Do not retrieve the ball for the opposition because that will save them time and energy. Sure, allowing them to win these small battles will not in many situations be detrimental to your team, nor will it lead to goals. However, a few times a season, these situations can turn into goals for the other team if they are paying better attention and are ready to act appropriately. **This is also an excellent opportunity for your team to catch their breath if they have been running a lot.** Simply holding the ball for a bit longer or dropping it to the ground so that the opposition has to spend time collecting it can buy your team some added physical and mental rest.

Next, if you want to kill time during the game, then passing between the defenders and midfielders on your team is a terrific way to do so. Granted, your team must have the talent to maintain possession. **Otherwise, in the last few minutes of the game, consider kicking the ball up the field or having one of your best players dribble the ball to the corner flag and prevent the other team from gaining possession.** Tactics like this may be considered a bit unsportsmanlike, but they are certainly within the rules of the game and should be considered when your team is looking for any advantage to run out the clock for a win.

In summary, use appropriate clock management techniques when you want to sustain a lead in a game. Avoid quickly giving the ball to the other team when it goes out of bounds. Instead, make them use their energy to get the ball and give yourself enough time to get into the proper position. Pass the ball extensively amongst your back line and midfielders to tire the other team's forwards and midfielders, as they are the players who will need the most energy to score towards the end of the game. Finally, when you are in an uncomfortable situation on the field, kick the ball past the other team's defenders or run the ball to the corner flag to delay the other team from gaining possession.

Chapter 15

Offside Trap, High Lines, and Low Lines

According to the Fédération Internationale de Football Association (FIFA), the governing body of soccer, a player is in an offside position if they are nearer to their opponents' goal line than both the ball and the second-to-last opponent. Offside occurs if the player is in an offside position at the same time as the ball is passed forward to them from the opposition's side of the pitch. **In simple terms, a player is offside when they receive the ball between the last defender and the goalkeeper while they are in the opposition's half of the field.**

The offside trap consists of the defenders traveling higher up the field than the attacking player just before the ball is passed. When done correctly, the offside trap allows the defending team to win the ball back without having to intercept a pass, block a shot, or make a tackle. The offside trap is a high-risk, high-reward tactic. If it is done properly, then the defense is awarded possession, but if there is even a small breakdown, then a failed offside trap can lead to an easy goal.

To implement the offside trap, you must generally have a flat (i.e., straight) back line and use a center back who can read the game and communicate loudly.

The defense must be ready to act quickly and in unison; otherwise, they will risk an opposing player being onside with few (if any) defenders between them and a shot-on-goal. This results in a relatively straight back line that is parallel to the goal line so that no single defender must move much farther than their teammates. It is okay for an outside defender to venture forward and become a part of the attack, but they must act as a unit with the other defensive backs when defending.

The center back must analyze the play as it develops in front of them and decide when to use the trap. The defender who is responsible for determining when to use the offside trap must know the location of their defending teammates and opposing forwards, while also understanding when the opponents will be likely to kick the ball forward. To achieve this, they should look for an attacking player who puts their head down before passing, and an attacking player who is making a run up the field near the back line. This is a vital defensive role because usually the entire defense will take their cues from the center back.

Due to the need for a defensive line that works as a unit and good judgment by the center back, **the offside trap is**

often used by experienced teams that have played together. If a few steps forward would suddenly make the striker offside, then the center back will move the defensive line up to win the free kick that is awarded because of the other team's offside. If the center back believes the opponents will play the ball before the defense can step up, then they will probably tell their teammates to drop back and take a defensive position. Having fast defenders and especially fast center backs are helpful when using the offside trap, so they can recover if an attacking player remains onside.

The offside trap is simple to understand but difficult to make it work consistently as one unit. The difficulty lies in coordinating, timing, and identifying those instances when the opposition will be ready to play the ball. If the defenders' communication and timing is not perfect, then there will be a high chance for an attacking player to make a breakaway. **Even if your team has perfected the offside trap, you will still come across a linesman or referee from time-to-time who will not call an offside—even if there was one.** Furthermore, if the offside trap is overused, then the opposing team will adapt their style to counter it.

To use the offside trap, your team cannot have a sweeper that is positioned deeper than the other defenders on the team. A sweeper will often ensure that the opposing player who is making a run will be onside when the ball is played. Therefore, the offside trap is best used with formations that do not use a sweeper.

As a defender, understanding how the offside trap can be defeated is important to help determine if it should be used in a specific instance. **First, if the opposing team has players who are good at using foot skills to travel past defenders, then they may beat the first defender and force the other defenders to cover in support.** The defending team's resulting disorganization will create lanes to dribble in or make a pass to an onside teammate.

Second, a team may use short passes to break an offside trap. If the defending team does not apply pressure on the player with the ball quickly enough, then the player who receives the short pass will have time to control the ball, look for a pass, and make a play to a nearby teammate.

Third, an offside trap is often ineffective against a team with a speedy striker. The striker will use their speed by running parallel to the defending line before the ball is played, at which point they will explode past the defenders. By using this tactic, they will give themselves several chances per game to score against the offside trap.

The team that is using the offside trap may also use a high defensive line. **A high defensive line is a high-risk (e.g.,** it frequently allows breakaways), high-reward (e.g., it creates many turnovers by the other team) style of play that involves a team pushing up the field to reduce the time that the opposition has to dribble or pass. Using a high defensive line reduces the size of the pitch by limiting the space and time in which the opposition can possess the ball. Having a high defensive line will leave plenty of space behind the defense for speedsters on the other team to collect the ball with few defenders to beat.

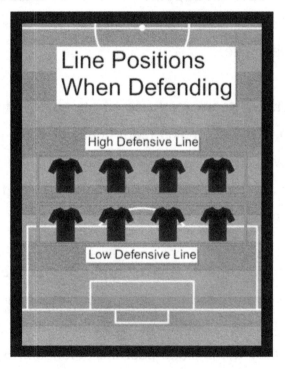

The low defensive line (also known as "the low block") is the opposite of the high defensive line. The low defensive line is a low-risk (e.g., fewer goals will be scored against it), low-reward (e.g., fewer turnovers will be created by the team who uses it) style of defending. The low defensive line is often used by teams with a good striker/center forward who can counterattack well or hold the ball effectively for their supporting teammates. The low defensive line is frequently implemented with the 5-4-1 formation and involves the defending team keeping the entire game in front of them by positioning themselves deep in their own zone. To read more about the 5-4-1 formation (and a dozen or so others) in order to determine which one is the best for your team, consider grabbing a copy of the *Understand Soccer* series book, *Soccer Coaching: A Step-by-Step Guide on How to Lead Your Players, Manage Parents, and Select the Best Formation*.

YouTube: If you would like to watch a video on the offside trap, then consider watching the *Understand Soccer* YouTube video: *Offside Trap in Soccer*.

Chapter 16

Receiving a Pass from Another Defender or the Goalkeeper

As a defender, you will often find yourself in high-pressure situations when you receive the ball. Knowing what to do and how to do it will take you from being a good defender to a *great* defender. The most important elements of a successfully received pass are:

1. Maintain proper positioning.
2. Scan and make a plan.
3. Open with the correct foot.
4. Know your step-over.

When determining how to position yourself to receive a pass from the goalkeeper or another defender, you must be wide enough while still being able to recover if a mistake occurs. Generally, you should maintain a wide position when your team has the ball, as this will allow the ball to work and force the other team to run. You should stay close together when the other team has the ball to avoid easily letting them easily pass through your team. Therefore, when your goalkeeper or defender has the ball, travel away from them to create space. Then, scan the field before yelling for the ball. Avoid asking for the ball if you are under pressure. Scanning the field will also allow you to determine what you should do next.

Next, use the foot that is facing the direction in which you are attacking to receive the ball. For example, if you are the leftmost defender and are receiving a pass from the goalkeeper, then you should take a moving first touch using your left foot, since you will be attacking to your left. Using your right foot would only cross your feet and increase the chance of an inaccurate touch.

Finally, realize that you do not have to win the game each time you receive the ball. Do not hesitate to pass the ball back to the person from whom you received it if you are not open, but they still are. However, there will be certain situations in which you will have the ball with significant pressure and cannot pass it to another defender or the goalkeeper. In this instance, use a step-over. **The step-over is best used when your back is facing the direction in which you need to go. Never use it when you are attacking an opposing player who is backpedaling.** Many soccer players mistakenly call a scissor a "step-over," but they are different. During a scissor, the foot closest to the ball goes around the ball. During a step-over, you are standing next to the ball, so the leg farthest from the ball should step over the ball. Then bring your other leg around to plant your legs on the opposite side of the ball and push the ball away with the leg that initially started the step-over.

To perform the step-over correctly, you must fully turn your shoulders in the direction you want the defender to believe you are going, thereby faking them and going in the opposite direction. A step over is an excellent way to fake out a defender when they are on your back. **The step-over makes them believe you are going in one direction, but then you intentionally miss the ball completely so that you can push it out and accelerate with speed in the opposite direction.**

In summary, start by adequately positioning yourself, so you can accurately scan the field. Receive the ball with the foot that is facing the direction in which you are attacking. Use a step-over when you have a defender on your backside while you are facing your own goal. Finally, understand that sometimes teammates will place you in a difficult situation. If you are ever uncertain about your best action, then kicking the ball out of bounds to provide time for more defenders to travel behind it is acceptable, too.

Chapter 17

Defending Tricks

This chapter reveals a few defending hacks that can make it easier to stop the other team from scoring. But remember that these little tricks are often as easy to do as they are *not* to do. Consider adding the following tactics to your game:

1. Call out the wrong time.
2. Learn how to pass back to the goalkeeper.
3. Being nutmegged is okay!
4. Learn how to defend as a forward.

If you are playing in a game with a scoreboard clock, then as the clock is running out, consider yelling out an incorrect amount of remaining time while the other team has the ball. **For example, if there are 15 seconds on the clock, and they are close to your net, consider yelling out, "6... 5... 4... 3... 2...1!"** This trick will often force the other team's player to avoid making a quality pass in favor of taking a rushed shot that has little-to-no chance of going in. Since they are dribbling with the ball, they will believe whatever you yell out because they know that looking at the clock themselves will take extra time. Plus, when a player receives the ball near the end of the half or the end of the game, they cannot mentally account for the amount of remaining time, coupled with what they need to do with the ball. This trick works so well that when I have yelled out the incorrect time, I have had several opponents take shots that are 30 or so yards from the net. These unrealistic shots were easy for the goalkeeper to stop and prevented the other team from scoring.

Next, when passing back to the goalkeeper, be sure to pass back across the frame of the net. **Specifically, pass the ball back so that even if the goalkeeper misses the ball, it will still go out of bounds along the end line and not into the back of your net.** Even at the professional level, many goals have been scored because of a poor pass back or because the goalkeeper mishandled the ball.

Furthermore, many players make the nutmeg seem like one of the most important things in soccer. Many feel that if you nutmeg someone, you have completely disrespected the other player, and therefore you are superior. In reality, a nutmeg is often a 50-50 chance because even if the ball goes through the defender's legs, there is a good chance that the dribbling player will not recover the ball. Therefore, do not be concerned with being nutmegged. Naturally, it is not fun to be nutmegged but being a good defender means preventing the other team from scoring. **Often, keeping your legs farther apart will give you a better chance to slow the attacking player because you will be taking up more space on the field, and therefore will**

be harder to travel around. Remember, the nutmeg does not count if the other team cannot maintain possession of the ball.

Additionally, when defending as a forward, you must first determine the opposing team's weakest player on their back line and use nearly all your effort to take advantage of them. Position yourself so that the opposing team must play the ball to the back line's weakest player. **Once the weakest player receives the ball, pounce on them and press them heavily.** Other defenders may also be easy to take the ball away from in certain situations, so be on the lookout! However, remember that your most frequent chances will come from their worst defender, so pressure them hard!

These tips are easy to implement and will make defending easier for you and your team. From calling out the wrong time to correctly passing back to the keeper, and from being okay with being nutmegged to attacking the weakest link, you should always look for opportunities to be the best defender you can.

YouTube: If you would like a video on a few tricks to use while defending, then consider watching the *Understand Soccer* YouTube video: *Soccer Defensive Tactics*.

Chapter 18

Defending Homework Assignment

"My ambition is always to get better and better."
–Lionel Messi

Perform this homework in an open area, such as in the backyard during your free time, before a game to warm up, or before your next practice. For those who want to develop their skills quicker, practice this 3-4 times in the upcoming week and complete it by the start of your next week's practice.

Easy Defending Rules to Remember:

1. P – Patience
2. A – Angled
3. T – Toes

Tips:

-Assume the attacker is right-footed, until you observe otherwise.

-Push the attacker to their weaker foot if they are in the middle of the field. Push them out of bounds if they are along a sideline.

-When the attacker turns their back to the net, be aggressive.

-Keep your arm/elbow up to make it easier to turn and to appear bigger.

-A good defender will decide where the attacker travels.

Homework:

      1. Run up to a ball and backpedal with an angled form for 20 yards, while pushing the attacker to their **left foot**. Do this four times, while focusing on an angled run to the ball.

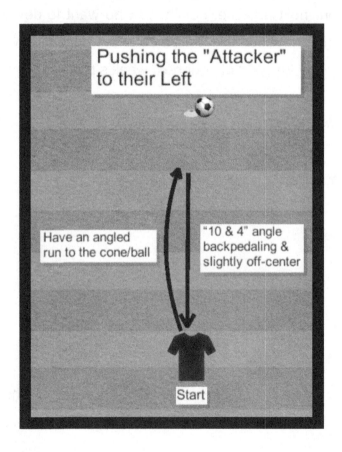

2. Run up to a ball and backpedal with an angled form for 20 yards, while pushing the attacker to their **right foot**. Do this four times, while focusing on an angled run to the ball.

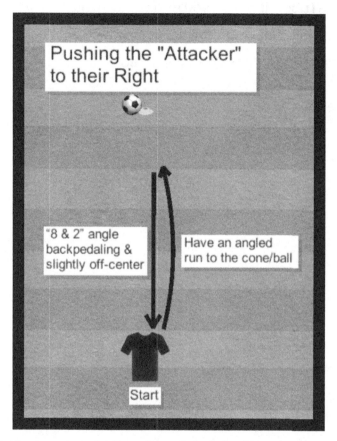

3. Run up to a ball and backpedal with an angled form for 20 yards. **Switch the direction in which you are pushing the attacker every five yards.** Do this four times, while focusing on an angled run to the ball.

Note: The above drills focus on approaching a cone (i.e., a defender) at an angle, using a balanced stance with the arm closest to the attacker raised. Ensure that you are off-center to force the attacker in the direction you want them to travel, while keeping your feet at "8 and 2" or "10 and 4" to push the attacker to their right and left, respectively.

YouTube: If you would like to watch a video of a defending drill that you can do alone, then consider watching the Understand Soccer YouTube video: *Defensive Soccer Drills to Do Alone*.

Soccer Positions:

A Step-by-Step Guide about Each Player on a Team

Introduction

The image details all the possible positions that a coach can assign to a player. Although it may seem overwhelming at first, remember that there are only 11 players on the field, and most formations will never use many of the positions shown. However, I have included them to provide a complete picture of all the options.

GK   Goalkeeper
SWP   Sweeper
RB   Right Back
RCB   Right Center Back
CB   Center Back
LCB   Left Center Back
LB   Left Back
RWB   Right Wing Back
STP   Stopper
LWB   Left Wing Back
RCDM   Right Center Defensive Midfielder
CDM   Center Defensive Midfielder
LCDM   Left Center Defensive Midfielder
RM   Right Midfielder
RCM   Right Center Midfielder
CM   Center Midfielder
LCM   Left Center Midfielder
LM   Left Midfielder
RCAM   Right Center Attacking Midfielder

CAM   Center Attacking Midfielder

LCAM   Left Center Attacking Midfielder

RW   Right Winger

LW   Left Winger

IR   Inside Right

F9   False Nine

IL   Inside Left

RF   Right Forward

CF   Center Forward

LF   Left Forward

ST   Striker

This book was written to help the reader understand each position's advantages and disadvantages. Although soccer positions are constantly evolving, this book will help a soccer player determine which position their skills would be best suited for, or which skills they need to develop to play their desired position. This book will also help coaches select which types of roles they want their players to fill, so they can get the most from each player on the team. Keep in mind that positions take on different roles, depending on the strategies and formations used by the coach.

If you are interested in several detailed chapters on all the different formations, as well as their variations, then grab a copy of the *Understand Soccer* series book, **Soccer Coaching:**

A Step-by-Step Guide on How to Lead Your Players, Manage Parents, and Select the Best Soccer Formation. This book will help you understand that there are three main formations in today's modern game. Think of these formations as the "Big Three" formations (i.e., 4-4-2, 4-5-1, and 4-3-3).

4-4-2 Formation

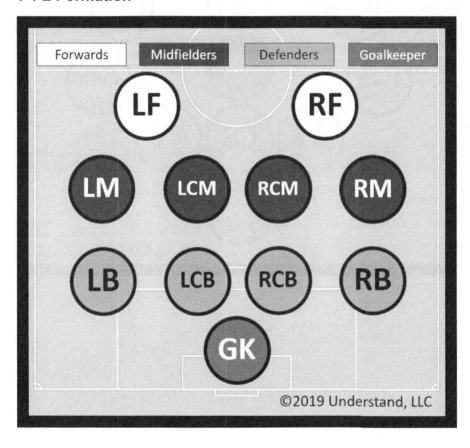

©2019 Understand, LLC

5-4-1 Formation

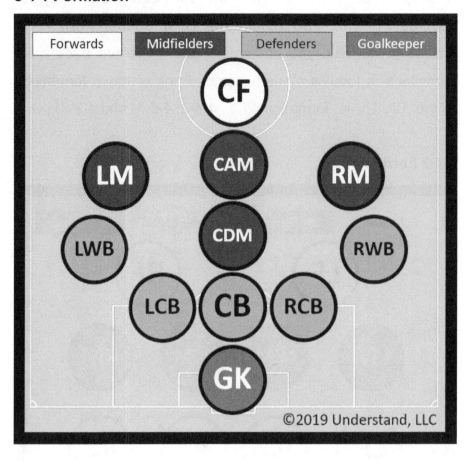

©2019 Understand, LLC

4-3-3 Formation

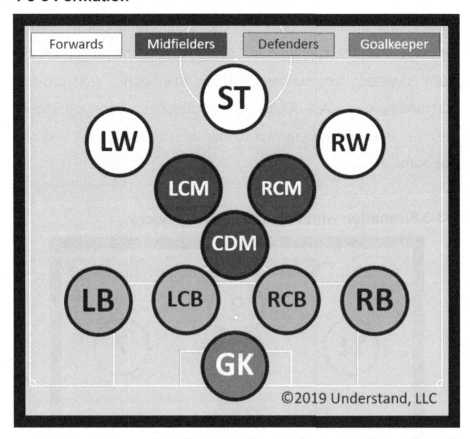

Forwards | Midfielders | Defenders | Goalkeeper

©2019 Understand, LLC

A good coach will assess their players' skills and their team's abilities against other teams. **A knowledgeable coach will know that forcing a preferred formation on a team that cannot handle it is a recipe for disaster. Understand that a great coach will pick their formation based on their players**, and not the other way around. Teams with very skilled players tend to want more forwards and favor the 4-3-3, whereas teams with fewer technical skills and good defenders will benefit from a 5-4-1.

Each chapter in this book, Soccer Positions, will recommend additional books in the *Understand Soccer* series for players or coaches who are seeking more instruction on the skills needed for success. Also, this book will provide outstanding examples of players and coaches whom you should watch and emulate if you would like to succeed in your desired position.

4-3-3 Formation with Player Jersey Numbers

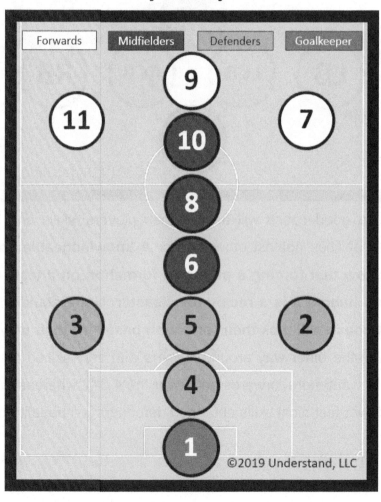

Often, when watching soccer, you will hear the commentator referencing different types of players as "numbers." Although not all teams use it, the standard numbering system for each position started in the 1920s. Numbering each player will help teach those who are still learning about soccer by creating an organized system in which to reference each player. In the image, the jersey numbers are shown using a 4-3-3 formation.

Lastly, this book, *Soccer Positions*, will reveal the traditional number for each player in each position on an 11-player team. Understand that a player's number is not limited to a certain position. A coach can place any number in any position they choose, and each position has different responsibilities to help the team win.

Please reference the glossary near the end of the book for definitions of words with which you are unfamiliar.

Chapter 1

Goalkeeper

Jersey Number: #1

The goalkeeper (also known as the "goalie" or "keeper") controls the 18-yard box, redirects or catches crosses, and prevents the other team from scoring. Goalkeepers wear a different-colored jersey than their team, the opposing team, and the officials. Common colors for a goalkeeper's jersey are black, blue, green, grey, and yellow. They often wear long-sleeved jerseys to protect their arms when diving for the ball, and pants with extra padding made for the position. Since the 1970s, goalkeepers have typically worn gloves to increase the size of their hands, prevent injuries to their hands from powerful shots, and make it easier to catch the ball and punch the ball out of the 18-yard box.

Goalkeepers are the only players on the team who are allowed to use their hands and arms to block shots and pick up the ball while it's in play. The advantage of using their hands only applies in their 18-yard box. Also, they cannot use their hands if a teammate used their feet to intentionally pass the ball to them during gameplay or a throw-in. If all other things are equal, then taller goalkeepers have a slight advantage because they can reach farther and cover more of the net.

The goalkeeper is the most defensive position in soccer because if a goalkeeper does not allow the ball into their net, their team cannot lose. Additionally, when the ball is in the goalkeeper's half, they have increased responsibilities to communicate with and direct their team to prevent the opposition from scoring. This can be while the ball is in play or during a set-piece for the other team.

A traditional goalkeeper (also known as a "shot-stopper") only focuses on preventing the ball from going into their net. They have great reflexes, quick instincts, and considerable agility. They have a limited role when it comes to being a part of attacks and often boot the ball down the field when it rolls to them to keep the ball safely out of their 18-yard box.

Considering the offside rule, having a defender act as a sweeper may be counterproductive if your team wants to catch the opposing players offside. However, in the last couple of decades, it has become commonplace for goalkeepers to assume the "sweeper" role. Modern goalkeepers are used as the starting point of many attacks. Whether they are throwing the ball up the field, kicking the ball to an open attacker, or passing the ball on the ground to a defender; goalkeepers are now more likely to have responsibilities besides keeping the ball out of the net. A sweeper-keeper (also known as a "sweeping goalkeeper") comes out of the net farther than a traditional keeper to help reduce the angle of a player's shot, to act as another field player to whom the defense can pass to maintain possession, and to prevent scoring opportunities by clearing passes and crosses outside the 18-yard box—and all without using their hands!

Skills Needed:

- Not afraid of a powerful shot
- Fast reaction time
- Can jump and dive repeatedly
- Good hands to catch or redirect the ball
- A powerful and accurate dominant foot to kick the ball far up the field during goal kicks and drop kicks
- Clear communication and a calm attitude
- A short memory when they make a mistake
- Ability to maintain focus in a game—even through long stretches of inactivity

Advantages:

- Wears gloves and is the only player who can use their hands in their 18-yard box (excluding throw-ins)
- Wears a different-colored outfit with more padding, thereby allowing their style and flair to shine
- Usually gets the glory in shutouts and shootouts when their team wins

Disadvantages:

- Takes responsibility for all goals against their team—even when it is not their fault
- Generally, does not receive glory for a win but receives criticism for a loss
- Is the least-transferable position because the skills required for a goalkeeper are significantly different than those required for a field player

Example Players:

Gianluigi Buffon – Paris Saint-Germain, Juventus, and the Italian National Team. Buffon was called up for a record of five FIFA World Cups in 1998, 2002, 2006, 2010, and 2014. He won the 2006 FIFA World Cup in Germany. He also represented Italy at four European Championships, at the 1996 Olympics, and at two FIFA Confederations Cups. He is a goalkeeper with incredible longevity. With an approximately 25-year career, he is someone whose form you should emulate to reduce the wear-and-tear injuries that so many goalkeepers face. His style of play is similar to that of a shot-stopper, as he does not contribute much to his team's offensive attacks.

"I've made a lot of mistakes in my life, but I think that's normal for someone who wants to grow and develop. You will have to overcome plenty of obstacles, and it is normal that you should stumble sometimes."—Gianluigi Buffon

Manuel Neuer - Bayern Munich and the German National Team. Neuer is considered to be the first in the new generation of "sweeper-keepers." He is a goalkeeper who will press up and act as a sweeper when the situation demands it. Additionally, when his team has possession, he is quick to distribute the ball, using techniques developed from playing as a midfielder in practice. Neuer has a plethora of hardware in his trophy cabinet. From Footballer of the Year to Champions League Winner, and from German League Champion to World Cup Winner, Neuer is one of the most decorated goalkeepers of all time.

"Take what's useful, leave out what's useless, and add a bit of yourself!"—Manuel Neuer

Chapter 2

Full Back

Jersey Number: #2 or #3

A full back is either the right back (i.e., right defender) or left back (i.e., left defender.) Full backs position themselves to either side of the center backs to limit the effectiveness of wide attackers on the opposing team. They will often cover outside forwards and wingers (depending on the formation used by the other team) to prevent crosses into the 18-yard box and to avoid the ball being dribbled in from the flank (i.e., the field's wide areas.)

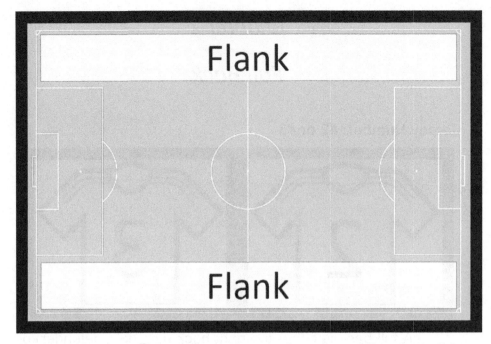

Full backs provide support for the right and left midfielders when they have been beat. They are also another option to pass to when under pressure. Full backs assist with protecting and helping their center backs, too.

Full backs rarely ever join the attack, like a wing back would. Excitingly, full backs are often the players who take throw-ins because they are along the sides of the fields, and coaches want the more skilled midfielders and forwards to receive the ball from a throw-in. Although the midfielders and forwards tend to be better at dribbling the ball, full backs need to be good at passing and receiving because their wide positioning makes them optimal to receive passes.

Full backs need to be fast to keep up with the wingers and outside midfielders on the other team. Although it is not as necessary as it is for a center back, it helps if a full back is also good at heading because they will often need to clear crosses out of their 18-yard box.

It is important that full backs understand how to position themselves in relation to attackers and other players on their team, while still tackling effectively and dispossessing the opposition when needed. Full backs need to understand when to engage the attacking player, and when to reduce pressure, as well. Since center backs and the goalkeeper often have good positions to view the field, they will often shout commands, and the full backs will need to be good at listening to their advice and act on it quickly.

Skills Needed:

- Good at headers
- Can tackle an attacker
- Tracking abilities
- Good at taking directions
- Quick pace

Advantages:

- Focus only on their major role of preventing the other team from scoring, unlike a wing back
- Takes throw-ins
- Often faster than the center backs because they need to shut down the quick wingers and outside midfielders

Disadvantages:

- Few opportunities to score or provide assists
- Wing backs who are more skilled with the ball are more preferred than full backs in today's style of play
- Generally, full backs do not receive the glory for a win but do receive the criticism for a loss

Example Players:

Paolo Maldini - AC Milan and the Italian National Team. Over the course of Maldini's 20+ year career, he has won several Champions Leagues, the Serie A on multiple occasions, and numerous Super Cups, too. He started as a full back and played a considerable amount of his career as a left back—even though he was right-footed—because he was so effective at shutting down the other team's dominant right-footed players. Maldini was so technical that he only made .56 tackles per game—which is unheard of for a defender at his level. He cared about beating the other team by mentally outwitting and out-positioning them, while most other defenders only attempt to overpower the other team.

"If I have to make a tackle, then I have already made a mistake."—Paulo Maldini

<u>Philipp Lahm</u> - Bayern Munich and the German National Team. To gain insight on the leader that Lahm was, consider that, as a defender, he was named captain of Bayern Munich. Bayern Munich has been the most consistent German team over the past two decades, with Philipp Lahm leading the charge for much of that time. Lahm has many of the most coveted trophies in soccer. From being a German Footballer of the Year to a World Cup Winner and Champions League Winner to winning every major trophy in Germany, Philipp Lahm has the winning attitude and drive that a full back needs.

"One of the reasons for my success at Bayern is the relationship with Philipp Lahm; he helped me a lot from the beginning. He always performs. I have never seen Philipp have a poor match. He will always be a special person in my life, and he is an absolute legend. Philipp Lahm is the most intelligent soccer player I have ever coached."—Pep Guardiola

YouTube: If you would like to see a video on the full back position, then consider watching the *Understand Soccer* YouTube video: _Full Back Positioning_.

Chapter 3

Wing Back

Jersey Number: #2 or #3

Note: These are the same numbers as a right full back and left full back.

As one of the most challenging soccer positions, a wing back plays on the sides of the center backs. This placement is similar to that of a full back because a wing back often has the same defensive responsibilities. However, a wing back also contributes to the team's attack. These "attacking full backs" work in the flanks, which is also where wingers can be found. The name "wing back" is a combination of "winger" and "full back."

Wing backs are more adventurous than full backs and can potentially act as the wingers on a team that is without wingers. This position allows for a considerable amount of width when attacking. Width is important to create gaps between defenders and increase the number of passing options. Due to their positioning in the flanks, wing backs must be good at crossing the ball. Wing backs help create coverage gaps because they line up as full backs but attack up the field, thereby making it difficult for opposing teams to decide who will cover them. Consider the below image to further understand the differences in field positioning between a full back (left full back) and a wing back (right wing back).

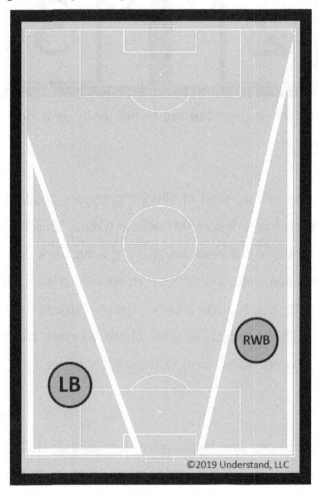

Wing backs must have great endurance because of their offensive and defensive responsibilities in what is one of the most physically demanding positions in modern soccer. However, a quality coach will pick a formation like a 5-3-2, which suits the use of a wing back. Otherwise, the coach may surround the wing back with a holding midfielder and outside midfielder, who can defend and help relieve some of the defensive requirements of a wing back. Wing backs are often a feature of teams who play with three center backs. If a team uses two wing backs, then the wing back on the side with the ball will be permitted to travel up the field and help with the attack, while the other must stay back and defend like a traditional full back.

Skills Needed:

- Can cross the ball into the 18-yard box
- Has a ton of stamina
- Can defend attacking players effectively
- Good at taking directions
- Can dribble at speed to travel past the other team
- Effective at communicating when they need help from teammates

Advantages:

- Focuses on preventing the other team from scoring and helping their team attack by providing assists
- Takes throw-ins

- Often faster than the center backs because they need to shut down the quick wingers and outside midfielders

Disadvantages:

- Must run a ton due to their offensive and defensive responsibilities
- Are often blamed for the other team's goals if they do not get back into a defensive position in time
- Although they are part of the attack, they rarely score because they play in the flanks

Example Players:

Dani Alves - Paris Saint-Germain, Juventus, Barcelona, and the Brazilian National Team. Dani is the definition of a hard worker. As a child, he used to wake up at 4 AM to help his father on the farm, and then he would spend most of the evening soccer training. His family could not afford to let Dani play for a club, so they assembled a team themselves to give him the opportunity to improve. This can-do attitude allowed him to win the Champions League multiple times, as well as the UEFA Cup, and the UEFA Super Cup. Also, he has won the league and cup title of all three major soccer nations he has played in (Spain, Italy, and France.) Alves is seen as an attacker placed in a defensive position. In fact, during his eight years with Barcelona, he had 102 assists as a wing back. That is 10 more assists than the famous attacking midfielder Zinedine Zidane had for both club and country.

"It would be difficult to find another like him."—Lionel Messi, when asked about Dani Alves' departure from Barcelona

Marcelo Vieira - Real Madrid and the Brazilian National Team. Many Brazilians are known only by one name. This is the case for Marcelo Vieira, who is largely known as "Marcelo." Having played for over a decade with Real Madrid and being the starting left wing back for the high-performing Brazilian National Team, Marcelo has been on the big stage all his adult life. However, as a child, Marcelo had no formal education and came from a very rough area. Playing soccer was the only thing he learned during his childhood because the soccer club he played in also doubled as his school. At one point, Marcelo almost had to quit soccer because he could not afford the bus to take him to training. However, his focus and drive helped him find a way onto the local club team before being signed by Real Madrid. Marcelo's never-quit attitude has allowed him to be one of the best wing backs of all-time. His work ethic has helped his team win numerous Champions Leagues, several La Liga titles, the Spanish Cup, and the Confederations Cup.

"The rule is: If you cannot get back [in time to support the defense], you must not go forward. The current best specialist is Marcelo, who gets it right in both areas."—Paolo Maldini

Chapter 4

Sweeper

Jersey Number: #4

The sweeper (also known as the "libero", which is Italian for "free") acts a defender with no marking responsibilities. They line up behind the other defenders and are free to disrupt the opposition however they please. A sweeper acts as a type of center-back who sweeps away the ball if an opponent manages to pass through or dribble past the line of defensive players.

The sweeper has fallen out of favor in recent years, as this position almost always ensures that you cannot catch the other team offsides when you have a roaming defender behind the line of defense. Sweepers are usually faster than other players and must be great at reading the game since they can roam wherever support is needed.

Because a sweeper can take possession of the ball by dispossessing an opposing dribbler—or more commonly, by cutting off a passing lane—they usually need good passing skills to create a quick counterattack. Since a sweeper is behind the other defenders, they often direct their teammates on what to do and who to mark, based on everyone's positioning, and the sweeper's vision of the field.

Skills Needed:

- Great vision and can read the game
- Fast reaction time
- Good defending skills
- Can pass the ball after dispossessing the other team
- Communication and leadership abilities
- Good at judging when to tackle

Advantages:

- Can roam to the portion of the defense where help is needed
- Often starts the counterattack
- Has the best defensive point-of-view, which allows them to direct the defense

Disadvantages:

- A mistake often becomes a goal for the other team
- Generally, they do not receive the glory for a win, but they do receive criticism for a loss

- Often prevents the other team from being caught offside

Example Players:

Franz Beckenbauer - Bayern Munich and the West German National Team. Nicknamed "The Emperor," he was regarded by many as the best sweeper of all-time and is credited with being the originator of this position. Beckenbauer was a two-time winner of the Ballon d'Or Award in 1972 and 1976. He is the only person in soccer history to have both captained and managed World Cup winning teams. He has won the Bundesliga, the UEFA Cup, and the UEFA European Football Championship, among other things. Being the first true libero, he also involved himself in the attack on numerous occasions. In fact, he even scored 14 goals internationally during his career—even though he was the player positioned closest to his own keeper.

"Soccer is one of the world's best means of communication. It is impartial, apolitical, and universal. Soccer unites people around the world every day. Young or old, players or fans, rich or poor, the game makes everyone equal, stirs the imagination, makes people happy, and makes them sad."— Franz Beckenbauer

Leonardo Bonucci - Juventus and the Italian National Team. Bonucci is an Italian Footballer of the Year, an Italian

Super Cup Winner, a Euro 2020 winner, and he has multiple Serie A league titles. In 2012, while browsing in a Ferrari dealership with his wife and son, a man whose face was covered approached Bonucci. He pointed a gun at Bonucci and demanded that the soccer player hand over his watch. Bonucci would have been wise to agree to the assailant's desires, but as the man went to take his watch, Bonucci punched him in the face, knocking him to the floor. Although this was a poor choice, and he would have been better off just handing over his watch, this is an example of his all-out relentless mindset and tough-as-nails character.

"One of my favorite ever players."—Pep Guardiola on Leonardo Bonucci

YouTube: If you would like to see a video on the sweeper position, then consider watching the *Understand Soccer* YouTube video: *Sweeper in Soccer*.

Chapter 5

Center Back/Stopper

Jersey Number: #5

Although in a formation, the "stopper" is positioned slightly in front of a center back, they largely serve the same function, so both will be discussed as one in this chapter. A center back is also referred to as the "center defender" or "center full back." Similar to the goalkeeper, the center back/stopper ensures that the other team does not score. Given that there are often a considerable amount of crosses into the 18-yard box, or clearances by the other team, the center back/stopper benefits from considerable height, size, strength, a high vertical leap, man-marking abilities, and consistency when heading the ball. Therefore, the center back/stopper is often one of the tallest (if not the tallest) players on the team.

Center backs generally use one of two defensive tactics to stop attackers. First, they may use zone coverage, which occurs when each center back handles a specific portion of the backfield. Otherwise, they may use man-to-man marking, which occurs when each center back manages one specific attacker on the other team. The man-to-man marking technique is more common for many soccer teams because it leaves no room for miscommunications regarding who covers each player. The zone-marking tactic requires defenders who can better read the game.

Center backs put their bodies on the line to make it as difficult as possible for the attackers on the opposing team. Center backs often push the boundaries of the game in terms of physical contact and they force the referees to consider making calls to keep the players safe. From hassling and annoying attackers to holding and tripping strikers, they may attempt to slow the other team in ways that are against the rules. Although center defenders will get calls against them, they will continue to frustrate the opposition—especially outside their own 18-yard penalty box.

Traditionally, center backs use to kick the ball up the field to keep it away from their net, but modern center backs often play a pivotal function in maintaining possession or finding passing lanes to midfielders or forwards.

Skills Needed:

- High vertical leap
- Considerable height and size
- Good at headers
- Can tackle an attacker
- Tracking abilities
- Good communication
- Accurate long passes

Advantages:

- A leader who is often the captain of the defense
- Large physical presence makes them difficult to get past in the air
- Frequently involved in the 18-yard box during set pieces and corner kicks on both sides of the field

Disadvantages:

- Takes responsibility for all goals against their team—even when it is not their fault
- Generally, center backs do not receive the glory for a win, but they do receive the criticism for a loss
- Often, they are not the fastest player because of their significant height and size

Example Players:

<u>Giorgio Chiellini</u> – Juventus and the Italian National Team. Chiellini, towering at 6'2", is an Italian superstar and Olympian. Chiellini is a 3X Defender of the Year in Serie A and has multiple league titles as part of Juventus. He recently won the Euro 2020, too. His demanding physical presence has forced forwards to retaliate in other ways to slow his game. From four broken noses to being bitten by Luis Suárez in the 2014 World Cup, Chiellini has taken abuse, as well as regularly dished it out.

"For me, the defender I respect the most is Giorgio Chiellini. He is one of the best defenders in the world. I really like the way he plays soccer on the pitch, the way he defends. He lives for the game. He transmits a sense of tranquility to his teammates. I have always admired his way to play."—Edinson Cavani

<u>Sergio Ramos</u> – Paris Saint-Germain, Real Madrid, and the Spanish National Team. Sergio Ramos is one of the most disliked players in the game. His physical style, in-your-face attitude, and additional ability to score big goals from set pieces in important games has only made the list of folks who dislike him even longer. His background includes amassing about 30 red cards, and in the 2018 Champions League Final, breaking the collarbone of Liverpool's star player, Mohamed Salah.

Within days of breaking Mohamed Salah's collarbone, over 500,000 people had signed a petition stating that Ramos was "an awful example to future generations" and urged soccer's governing bodies to punish him retroactively. Although he is not a great role model based on his antics, his abilities to perform when an important game is on the line and to be an overbearing defender in the backfield have allowed him to play for one of the best teams in the world for over a decade. Additionally, he has won a World Cup, multiple Champions Leagues, and about every worthwhile top-flight soccer competition in Spain.

"Nothing fills me more than the feeling of having given everything."—Sergio Ramos

Defending Summary

Defenders need to remember to focus on their main responsibility—specifically, to prevent the other team from scoring. One way to do this is with proper body positioning. **As a defender, your body positioning should be angled.** You should never point (i.e., "square") your hips at the attacker completely, because then it will allow the attacker to go to the right of you, to the left of you, or between your legs. You should be angled but not entirely turned to the side. Position one of your sides so that it faces the attacker but is still at a diagonal. If your feet were hands on a clock, then they should be positioned at either "10 and 4," (as shown in the first image) or "8 and 2," (as shown in the second image.)

This body positioning will allow you to push them either to the left or the right. **Standing at "10 and 4" will push them to their left foot and standing at "8 and 2" will push them to their right foot.** Keep in mind that just standing directly in front of them and turning your hips will not force them in the direction that you want them to go. You must be slightly off-center, with your hips set at either "10 and 4" or "8 and 2," to push them in the direction that you want them to go. If you just turn your hips directly in front of a good dribbler, then they will attack the side that you are not facing, which will make it easier for them to go around you. This will force you to turn farther to pursue them.

The above excerpt from the *Understand Soccer* series book, ***Soccer Defending: A Step-by-Step Guide on How to Stop the Other Team***, reveals that it is best to position yourself slightly closer to the side in which you do not want the attacker to go. If they attack in the direction in which you are forcing them to go, then your positioning will make it easier for you to tackle or pursue.

Chapter 6

Defensive/Holding Midfielder

Jersey Number: #6

Originally, midfielders were referred to as "half backs" because half their role was to play defense, and the other half was to play offense. Defensive midfielders are center midfielders who specialize in dispossessing the other team and cutting off passing lanes. Of all the midfield players, the defensive/holding midfielder is often viewed as the "ball winner." A ball winner is a soccer player who focuses on winning the ball back from the other team by intercepting it or making defensive challenges and the occasional tackle. This attribute almost always describes a defender. Putting this label on a midfielder signifies that they are the team's defensive center midfielder (also known as the "pivot").

A defensive midfielder is positioned just behind the center midfielder. Defensive midfielders allow the other center midfielder to focus more on attacking. When their team has the ball, defensive midfielders connect the defense to the midfield by moving the ball from one to the other. When the other team has the ball, they are tasked to prevent the ball from reaching the defense.

Passing and receiving skills are a must since they are in a crowded portion of the field. They must control a pass and distribute it to the open player. Therefore, holding midfielders can also make effective deep-lying playmakers. Deep-lying playmakers are players who position themselves near their team's defense, but because of their strong long-distance passing abilities, they can create quick attacking opportunities by playing the ball past many of the opposing players with just one pass.

Holding midfielders must be good tacklers, great at positioning themselves to cut off passes, and have a significant amount of endurance. Often, holding midfielders push attacking players towards the sidelines of the field to reduce the opposition's chances of creating dangerous plays and scoring. Holding midfielders are required to cover their defensive teammates when they have gone up the field to help the attack, which is often the case if the team uses a wing back. Holding midfielders slow the other team's speed of play and are often required to cover the opposition's best midfield player.

Skills Needed:

- Can tackle an attacker
- Passing and receiving in the part of the field with the most pressure
- Good at taking and giving directions
- Significant endurance
- Can shoot from outside the 18-yard box
- Knows when to commit a tactical foul

Advantages:

- Has mobility and can go wherever the situation demands
- Occasionally provide assists
- Helps prevent counterattacks from the other team

Disadvantages:

- Generally, does not score many goals
- Needs stamina and endurance because they tend to be one of the players who run the most
- Plays in the most congested portion of the field, which prevents much dribbling

Example Players:

N'Golo Kanté - Chelsea, Leicester, and the French National Team. Kanté is a relative newcomer to the soccer scene but has made a tremendous impact in a very short time. He was the engine behind Leicester City's famous title run, a team with 5000:1 odds at the beginning of the season to win the English Premier League. He has won the World Cup, French Footballer of the Year, the FA Cup, and back-to-back EPL titles. His quick rise to soccer stardom has resulted in humorous and untrue statements, known as "Kanté Facts." A few of the best are "the Earth is covered 70% by water, and the rest by Kanté," "Kanté can tackle your imaginary friends," and "Kanté once ran the London Marathon as a warm-up before a game." All these fake but funny quotes help describe the wealth of energy and endurance that Kanté uses in every game.

"This player, Kanté, he was running so hard that I thought he must have a pack full of batteries hidden in his shorts. He never stopped running in training. I tell him, 'One day, I am going to see you cross the ball, and then finish the cross with a header yourself.' He is unbelievable."—Claudio Ranieri

Sergio Busquets – Barcelona and the Spanish National Team. Being a tall and slow player, Busquets was not considered one of the best for many years—until the soccer world finally realized why Pep Guardiola brought him in. He has endurance, intelligence, and no desire to be recognized. One downfall of most holding midfielders is their need to seek the instant adoration and fame from fans when they score goals for their team. However, not playing this role properly forms a void in the midfield that many selfish defensive midfielders have demonstrated. Busquets is uninterested in the public's praise; he is only interested in helping his team win by playing as the best holding midfielder that he can possibly be. Busquets has quite the résumé. He has won the Euros, every meaningful Spanish title imaginable, the World Cup, and the Champions League on multiple occasions.

"I play in a position that demands hard work, and generosity, and little glamour, but I like it. It is my job, and I like it. I would rather intercept and steal 10 balls than shoot. That is what I am here for—to make everyone else's jobs easier."— Sergio Busquets

YouTube: If you would like to see a video on the holding midfielder position, then consider watching the *Understand Soccer* YouTube video: *Defensive Midfielder Positioning*.

Chapter 7

Outside Midfielder

Jersey Number: **Right Midfielder - #7**

Left Midfielder - #11

Traditionally known as a "left half" or "right half," outside midfielders are midfielders positioned to the right and left of the center midfielders. Outside midfielders provide width in the midfield. Width allows them to create space on the field by pulling the opponent's defense to the outside, so they can open lanes for their offense.

Having two outside midfielders, along with two center midfielders, means that the team is defensive-minded and willing to reduce some of their attacking power to prevent the other team from scoring. Conversely, having two wingers, instead of two outside midfielders, means that the team is giving the full backs less defensive support and is instead emphasizing the attack.

An outside midfielder's responsibilities are largely to cross balls into the 18-yard box and prevent the other team's outside midfielders/wing backs from being effective during the opposing team's attack. To shoot or cross the ball into the 18-yard box, one-on-one skills are helpful. However, outside midfielders have less shooting responsibilities. When they do shoot, most of their shots come from the edge of the 18-yard box and from crosses from the other side of the field. Because of outside midfielders' offensive and defensive responsibilities, and because they are in the uncrowded flanks, they will need considerable stamina. Additionally, due to their positioning in the flanks, outside midfielders should be open to and good at receiving directions from other players. They often do not have as good of a view as center midfielders or defenders, so they would be wise to act on the directions of their teammates.

Skills Needed:

- Considerable stamina
- Foot skills to travel past opposing players to cross the ball or shoot
- Effective at crossing the ball into the 18-yard box
- Can defend and close the other team's passing lanes
- A powerful and accurate shot
- Receptive to directions from teammates

Advantages:

- Offensive responsibilities to help their team score, which can result in goals or assists
- Since the outside midfielders work in the flanks, mistakes made by them are unlikely to result directly in a goal
- Great endurance

Disadvantages:

- Must balance defensive and offensive responsibilities, unlike a predominately offensive winger
- Generally, does not have many opportunities with the ball each game, which also limits their chances to score
- Since the flanks have more space than any other portion of the field, a mistake with the ball may result in no nearby teammates who can help win the ball back

Example Players:

Philippe Coutinho – Barcelona, Liverpool, Inter Milan, and the Brazilian National Team. As a Spanish Champion, Italian and Spanish Cup Winner, Under-20 World Cup Champion, and Italian and Spanish Super Cup Winner, he is a good outside midfielder, who sometimes lines up as a winger, given his abilities to dribble and shoot. Coutinho is a student of the game who understands that becoming better is a process and takes time. He and his two brothers watch and break down each of Philippe's games to help improve his latest performance. This dedication reveals why he has had success in three of the top leagues in Europe.

"I see soccer as a bit like a stairway. You have to climb it bit by bit. First, you have to play good soccer so that you get to play for a good team. Then hopefully, you achieve such a level that you are invited to play for your national side in time for a World Cup."—Philippe Coutinho

David Beckham - LA Galaxy, Paris Saint-Germain, Real Madrid, Manchester United, and the English National Team. For many passive soccer watchers, David Beckham is one of the most recognized names in soccer. Due to his conventional good looks, and his marriage to one of the Spice Girls, he created a huge brand for himself that crossed the barrier between soccer and mainstream media. However, all the media popularity was a result of his nonstop work ethic in soccer. Given that Beckham was an outside midfielder, he became top of the class with his dangerous free kicks and crosses. He could achieve so much curve with the ball that many soccer fans refer to a player who can curve the ball as being able to "bend it like Beckham." His nonstop running and wonderful crosses helped him become a Champions League Winner and the Best Player in Europe. Seemingly, whichever country he went to, he became a champion. This includes England, Spain, France, and even the

United States of America. From FA Cups to Super Cups, and even Intercontinental Cups, Beckham has a decorated tenure in professional soccer.

"The only time you run out of chances is when you stop taking them."—David Beckham

Chapter 8

Center/Box-to-Box Midfielder

Jersey Number: #8

A center midfielder is in the middle of the team. Center midfielders are surrounded by the offense and defense of both teams and are shoulder-to-shoulder with the midfielders of the opposing team. Therefore, they must be skilled with the ball in the most congested portion of the field. They have similar scoring responsibilities as an attacking midfielder, and similar goal-preventing responsibilities as a defensive midfielder. They also provide help when defending set pieces and must tackle properly to dispossess the other team. Due to their responsibilities on both sides of the ball, the box-to-box midfielders often have the most endurance of any player on the team.

A center midfielder is an important starting point of attack for a team. Center midfielders tend to be "playmakers" who distribute the ball to the attacking players after having moved it past most of the midfielders and some defenders. It is vital that they have exceptional passing skills and great vision of the field to understand the movements of their teammates and the opposing team.

When attacking, they often take shots from outside the 18-yard box to help their team score. Since a considerable amount of the game occurs in their portion of the field, midfielders often exert the greatest influence over a match. This is because the team that controls the middle third of the field is often the team that wins the game.

Skills Needed:

- Considerable endurance
- Accurate passes
- Excellent first touch
- Can dribble with a considerable amount of pressure
- Control over gameplay and flow
- Can shoot from outside the 18-yard box
- Leadership skills

Advantages:

- Usually handles the ball the most
- Provides many assists

- Usually, they are team leaders and are almost always a part of the play, due to their central position, and their defensive and offensive responsibilities

Disadvantages:

- Needs a considerable amount of endurance to play both defensively and offensively
- Must manage the different personalities of each player on the team
- Often passes the ball before they can shoot

Example Players:

Luka Modrić - Real Madrid, Tottenham, and the Croatian National Team. Modrić was born during the Croatian War of Independence, and although he did not partake in the conflict himself, he had family members whose lives were taken because of it. He attributes his strong work ethic and confidence to being raised in this horrifying experience. This tough-as-nails mentality allowed him to dethrone a decade of Messi and Ronaldo as FIFA Ballon d'Or Winners. Additionally, his outstanding effort and endless stamina allowed him to win the Best Player Award in the 2018 World Cup—even though he was on the losing team in the Finals. From winning the UEFA Best Player in Europe Award and multiple Player of the Year Awards in Croatia, to several Champions League victories and league titles in Croatia and Spain, he has a high-profile trophy case to contrast his modest and humble personality.

"The most important thing is to never give up, never give in to the circumstances, believe in yourself, and to soldier on, no matter what is in your way."—Luka Modrić

Paul Pogba – Manchester United, Juventus, and the French National Team. Pogba grew up in Paris with two brothers, who now play for the Guinea National Team. All three of them were very competitive and pushed each other to succeed in soccer. Their love for soccer was helped tremendously by their mother, who supported their soccer ambitions. Pogba is known for his pinpoint-accurate passing and flair for the game. These attributes have allowed him to win the World Cup and the Europa League, while attracting a €105M transfer fee in 2016—the largest ever at the time. Furthermore, he has an English League Cup victory, and many Italian trophies to his name.

"I only think about the pitch. I want to do great. I want to be one of the best. I want to win titles. I want to achieve things."—Paul Pogba

YouTube: If you would like to see a video on the center midfielder position, then consider watching the *Understand Soccer* YouTube video: *What is a Box-to-Box Midfielder*.

Chapter 9

Attacking Midfielder

Jersey Number: #10

An attacking midfielder is sometimes referred to as the "center attacking midfielder (CAM)," "creative midfielder," or "playmaker." They are stationed ahead of the rest of the midfield and behind the forwards. They tend to act as the main distributor of the ball, the initiator of most attacks, and they are considered by many to be the "soccer coach" on the field. Many soccer fans consider the #10 jersey to be the most prestigious jersey on the field, and it is often given to the best attacking player on the team—sometimes, even when they do not play attacking center midfielder.

An attacking midfielder's primary job is to collect the ball from other midfielders and defenders on the team. Therefore, they must control the pass and take a quality first-touch. The attacking center midfielder looks to where their teammates are positioned—often before they even receive the pass. From there, they judge whether to pass the ball to a teammate who has a better chance of progressing the play or to keep the ball and dribble themselves. Even a well-organized defense can be torn apart with an attacking center midfielder's vision and creativity.

Next, as the play develops, the attacking center midfielder constantly looks for a teammate to pass to, and when nearing the outside of the 18-yard box, they begin to think about shooting the ball, too. The better the attacking center midfielder, the more players from the other team they will draw towards them, thereby creating opportunities for their teammates to score. Due to their positioning on the field, attacking center midfielders and center forwards are often said to be "playing in the hole" of the opposing team's defense.

Attacking midfielders are often allowed a great deal of freedom to travel where they deem appropriate on the field. Their shifty movements can make it difficult for defenders to mark everyone appropriately, thereby creating havoc for the other team. All these responsibilities mean that attacking midfielders need to have strong stamina.

Additionally, an attacking midfielder may act as a second striker. In this role, the attacking midfielder acts as a supporting striker who can both score goals and distribute the ball to teammates who are making a run.

When a team uses an attacking center midfielder, they are usually paired with a defensive midfielder who focuses on preventing the other team from scoring. You will rarely see a player positioned as a false nine (discussed in a later chapter), an attacking midfielder, and a center midfielder on the same team.

Remember, the attacking midfielder is still a part of the midfield, and therefore they must have some defensive responsibilities. They must look to cut off passing lanes through the most dangerous part of the field—the middle. Attacking midfielders also need to position themselves well to prevent the other team from using their midfielders to start attacks.

Skills Needed:

- Can shoot from outside the 18-yard box
- Great at finding short-and-long-distance passing lanes and excellent at passing the ball
- Can control the ball and dribble with pressure from many opponents
- Great endurance
- Communicates, acts, and leads as the coach on the field

Advantages:

- A team leader who directs the attack
- Plenty of opportunities for assists and to score goals
- Often one of the best dribblers on the team, with the freedom to travel wherever they feel they can help the team score

Disadvantages:

- With leadership comes responsibility, which means taking some of the blame for losses
- Often helps start the offensive play but does not always get the assist or goal
- Surrounded by many players from both teams, so they are constantly under pressure

Example Players:

Zinedine Zidane - Real Madrid and the French National Team. Zidane (also known as "Zizou") is arguably France's greatest soccer player ever. Although he is known as a bit of a hothead—especially after he headbutted a player in the World Cup Finals—he is a leader on his team and is beloved by many around the world. Zidane was born in the French coastal town of Marseille and was the son of Algerian immigrants. He started playing soccer in the alleys of a rough section of town. As a player, he went on to win the Ballon d'Or three times, the

Champions League, the Euros, and even the World Cup—and these were only his on-the-field awards and trophies. He did the unimaginable by becoming Real Madrid's coach and won three straight Champions League titles—a feat that had never been accomplished before by a manager. He took a season off from coaching Real Madrid after winning the third trophy and is regarded by many to be the best all-around soccer star of all-time, considering his performances as both a player and coach.

"If you are determined and confident, there is nothing in this great existence that can stop you from achieving what you want."—Zinedine Zidane

<u>Johan Cruyff</u> – Barcelona, Ajax, and the Dutch National Team. Born in Amsterdam, Cruyff was very talented and hard-working from the start. At a young age, he was picked up by the Dutch powerhouse team, Ajax. Cruyff was the face behind the Netherlands' "Total Football," in which each player could play every position—and often did. Johan dazzled with his skills so much that he even has a skill named after him—the Cruyff. (See the third book in the *Understand Soccer* series, ***Soccer Dribbling & Foot Skills: A Step-by-Step Guide on How to Dribble Past the Other Team***, for an in-depth explanation of how to perform this skill along with many other skills. Additionally, it points out which skills that most players are taught that should be avoided.)

Cruyff has been named the Best Player in Europe, Footballer of the Year, and Top Scorer. Additionally, he is a Dutch and Spanish Champion who has won the UEFA Super Cup and Intercontinental Cup.

"You have got to shoot; otherwise, you cannot score."— Johan Cruyff

YouTube: If you would like to see a video on the attacking midfielder position, then consider watching the *Understand Soccer* YouTube video: *How to Play CAM in Soccer*.

Midfield Summary

Midfielders are the most versatile field players on the team. Due to their defensive and offensive roles, they must have skills in both departments to be effective. One area that makes a huge difference is their ability to move the ball from the defense to the offense. In the *Understand Soccer* series book, ***Soccer Passing & Receiving: A Step-by-Step Guide on How to Work with Your Teammates***, the form for an inside-of-a-foot pass, among other topics, is broken down step-by-step, as follows:

1. Plant next to the ball, while pointing your foot and hips at your teammate

2. Keep your toe up, heel down, and ankle locked

3. Keep your knees slightly bent and foot slightly off the ground

4. Follow through after making contact with the ball

Additionally, a midfielder will find themselves surrounded by multiple opponents nearly the entire game. Therefore, midfielders must have a few effective foot skills that they are comfortable using to ensure that they can keep the ball safe. The following are the Tier 2 foot skills. To learn the Tier 1 foot skills, consider grabbing a copy of the *Understand Soccer* series book, **Soccer Dribbling & Foot Skills: A Step-by-Step Guide on How to Dribble Past the Other Team**, where the best skills for each game situation are revealed.

Chapter 10

False Nine

Jersey Number: #9

Understand that this is an uncommon role, and 99% of coaches will never use this position. However, it can be a huge benefit to a team that has an all-star player, or a team that cannot create enough space to score. A false nine is a soccer player who is positioned as a center forward. Since center forwards are often given the #9 jersey, this is where the "nine" in false nine comes from. The difference between a false nine and a center forward (i.e., a true nine) is that the false nine will play more like an attacking midfielder. This means they will drop deeper towards their net than a center forward would. This allows them to both open lanes for wingers to cut in and to help pull a defender off the defensive/back line.

Most teams will make sure that each of the opposing team's forwards/strikers are man-marked. Therefore, they will assign one specific defender to them. Thus, if a false nine acts more like an attacking midfielder, then it forces the defender to make a choice. The defender may either leave the back line, which will create space for the false nine's teammates, or they can stay at the back line, but this will increase the likelihood of no one covering the false nine.

Center forwards usually position themselves next to the deepest defender. By doing this, they can vertically stretch the pitch and spread the opposing team. This creates larger gaps, which increases the chance to score. The coach who implements a 4-4-2 formation (i.e., four defenders, four midfielders, and two forwards) with a striker and center forward, or two center forwards, is assuming that their forwards are better than the defenders who are covering them, thereby giving them the advantage to score.

The false nine is more commonly found in the Latin American and Spanish preferred 4-3-3 formation, in which there are four defenders, three midfielders, and three forwards. Using the false nine requires a very skilled player with considerable soccer intelligence, who has the vision to unlock space in the defense. Since a false nine is positioned as a "forward," they must still score goals, but they share goal-scoring responsibilities with wingers.

Skills Needed:

- Vision to pass around the opposition's defenders
- Fast reaction time
- Outstanding foot skills
- Can score
- Can pass well

Advantages:

- Creates havoc for the defense to determine who should mark them
- Accumulates many goals and assists over the course of a season
- Often the most technical player on the team

Disadvantages:

- Takes responsibility when their team does not score
- Must have the soccer intelligence to know when to drop into the midfield versus when to attack
- Since there is no obvious opposing player to mark them, they may be covered by two players at once, which is a disadvantage for the false nine as an individual but beneficial to the false nine's team

Example Players:

Francesco Totti - Roma and the Italian National Team. Although he does not have as many trophies as the other players in this book, he has a love for his team like no one else. Raised in Rome, he only dreamed of playing for Roma, and he ended up doing so for all of his senior career. Although Roma is a great team, it is outstanding that he did not chase money and trophies by transferring to a more prestigious team, yet still managed to win several trophies and awards, including the Top Scorer Award, Footballer of the Year, the European Under-21 Championship, and the World Cup. In Italy, he has won the Serie A, the Italian Cup, and the Italian Super Cup.

"Francesco Totti is impressive. He is an example for all, and someone we all look up to. He shows that age is not important in soccer. If you feel good, you enjoy it. If you play at the level he does, it is good for him, for soccer, and also for the children because we give them the idea that soccer has no limits."—Cristiano Ronaldo

Lionel Messi - Paris Saint-Germain, Barcelona, and the Argentinian National Team. Although Messi can play many roles—and he has—he is included as a false nine in this book because of his time under Pep Guardiola. Frankly, Messi can be placed in any attacking position and still be considered one of the greatest of all-time. At an early age, Messi was diagnosed with a growth hormone deficiency. At age 13, he moved from Argentina to Spain to play for Barcelona, in large part because they agreed to pay for his medical treatments. He quickly grew in their youth academy and made his senior team debut at 17 years old.

During the 2010-11 campaign, Pep Guardiola decided to use Lionel Messi as a false nine, similar to how the Roma coach, Luciano Spalletti, used Francesco Totti. Messi did not have the size or strength to use his body against the defenders like a traditional forward, but he was too good a player to not be centrally located on the field. Pep feared using him in the midfield because a designated player would mark him, and the midfield is the most congested portion of the field. This genius idea allowed Messi to lead the attack and win the treble for Barcelona. Messi is one of the most decorated players of all-time. With multiple Ballon d'Ors, Best Player in Europe, Top Scorer, and Player of the Year, it is easy to see why he has so many fans. Aside from his personal achievements, this Olympian has also won several Champions Leagues, Spanish Championships, Spanish Cups, and Spanish Super Cups. Additionally, he has won the Club World Cup, the Under-20 World Cup, and the UEFA Super Cup.

"I start early, and I stay late, day after day, year after year. It took me 17 years and 114 days to become an overnight sensation."—Lionel Messi

YouTube: To see a video on the false nine position, then watch the *Understand Soccer* YouTube video: _False Nine_.

Chapter 11

Winger

Jersey Number: **Right Winger - #7**

Left Winger - #11

Note: *These are the same numbers as the right midfielder and left midfielder.*

Wingers aim to use their positioning to help increase the space between defenders. Wingers send crosses into the 18-yard box and finish them from the other winger on the opposite side of the field. Wingers attack the opponent's full backs and travel behind the defense, thereby making it easy to cross the ball towards the center for their attacking teammates to score.

Modern soccer is seeing a huge surge in wingers who dribble defenders and shoot. Since they play in the flanks, the wingers' opposition are usually the other team's full backs. Their role is like that of outside midfielders—except wingers play a bit farther up the field and are expected to score significantly more.

Look at the image to further understand the difference in field positioning between an outside midfielder (i.e., left midfielder) and a winger (i.e., right winger).

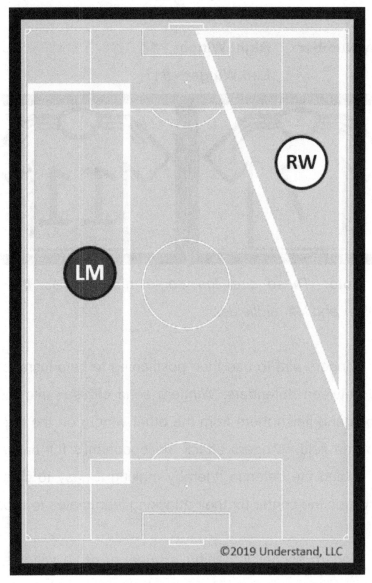

©2019 Understand, LLC

Due to their increased role in producing goals, they are not always required to track back quickly to help their defenders. Often, a team's winger is one of their fastest players on the field and covers the least crowded area of the field. Since they play in the less crowded flanks, they are expected to be great options to whom their teammates can pass the ball. In Latin and Dutch soccer countries, wingers usually play more like two outside forwards, as part of a 4-3-3 formation. However, the 4-4-2 is more prevalent in English-speaking countries, and the wingers are essentially the two outside midfielders.

Wingers generally function in one of two ways: Either they are an "out-and-out winger," or an "inside winger." The traditional winger is an out-and-out winger who positions themselves in the flanks. They use their speed to travel past the opposition's full backs, and they cross the ball to deliver solid passes to attacking teammates.

While many wingers prefer to stay out wide and travel in behind the full back, others act as an inverted/inside winger and dribble towards the net, either to pass a through ball to the striker or to shoot the ball themselves, often from outside the 18-yard box. Inverted wingers who want to cut in and shoot often line up on the side opposite their dominant foot. For example, if they are right-footed, then they take the position of a left winger to cut across the top of the 18-yard box to shoot. Many of the world's biggest clubs (e.g., Barcelona, Real Madrid, and Bayern Munich) play their wingers on the opposite side. Both examples of players included at the end of this chapter are considered to be "inverted wingers" because the out-and-out winger is a dying breed. Talented wingers want to share goal-scoring and not only contribute via assists from crosses on the wings.

Skills Needed:

- Speed and agility
- Can cross the ball accurately
- Can dribble defenders
- Takes accurate shots from a distance
- Has a considerable amount of endurance
- Receives passes and quickly accelerates the ball up the field

Advantages:

- Quick and skilled at taking on players in 1v1 situations
- Can shoot the ball powerfully from outside the 18-yard box
- Has a considerable amount of space in the flanks

Disadvantages:

- Does not get as many touches because they are off to one side and often away from the play
- A considerable amount of running—especially when the coach expects them to track back on defense

- Sometimes expected to only play as out-and-out wingers and contribute crosses into the 18-yard box, leaving little room for taking shots themselves

Example Players:

Arjen Robben – Chelsea, Real Madrid, Bayern Munich, and the Dutch National Team. Robben is an inside winger who controls the right flank and creates enough room to cut in and shoot with his left foot. When many people think of Robben, they only think of his ability to cut in and shoot towards the far post, as this is how nearly all his goals are scored. Considered to be a "glass man" because of his injuries early in his career, Robben has traveled around many of the major European teams and won each specific country's league. He has done this in the Netherlands, Spain, England, and Germany. Additionally, he has a UEFA Super Cup to his name, as well as Player of the Year and Footballer of the Year in the leagues he competed in.

"The best thing about soccer—and sports in general—is that if you suffer a big disappointment, there is no better feeling than coming back the following year and doing well."—Arjen Robben

Cristiano Ronaldo - Juventus, Real Madrid, Manchester United, and the Portuguese National Team. Ronaldo is an inside winger who loves to play the left wing to cut in and shoot with his dangerous right foot. However, his versatile skillset allows him to play in any attacking position that he desires. Ronaldo's swift pace—coupled with his ability to shoot from a distance—makes him hard to cover. Additionally, he is effective at dribbling a defender—and even more effective at heading in the ball. When it comes to awards, Ronaldo is among the top 5 all-time players. It is hard to consider where to start when looking at his history of winning. He is a multiple Ballon d'Or winner, and roughly the 20X top scorer in his league throughout his career. He has numerous Super Cups, has won a handful of Champions Leagues, lifted the 2016 European Championship, and is a league winner in England, Spain, and Italy. Also, Ronaldo captained the first-ever team to win the UEFA Nations League Cup.

"Talent without working hard is nothing."—Cristiano Ronaldo

YouTube: If you would like to see a video on the winger position, then consider watching the *Understand Soccer* YouTube video: *Soccer Winger Movement*.

Chapter 12

Forward

Jersey Number: #9

Traditionally, center forwards were required to be tall and physically strong to win the ball. A center forward is often man-marked by at least one player and has two players covering them. Due to their large stature, they are often responsible for five main jobs: (1) receiving clearances, (2) holding the ball, (3) making passes to strikers and wingers, (4) poaching goals from headers, and (5) contributing powerful long-range strikes.

The terms "center forward" and "striker" are often used interchangeably. However, center forwards are really "second strikers," whose positioning is behind a striker. They are big physical presences, whereas strikers tend to be speedsters who can dribble past defenders with ease.

A forward who can control clearances will allow a team to boot the ball out of their defense because they know that their point man (i.e., the forward) can handle the ball. Kicking the ball over the midfielders will reduce the chance of mistakes—and will especially reduce the amount of time that the opposing team has to get into their defensive position. A forward needs to use their size to hold the ball, while wingers and midfielders travel up the field to assist the attack. Once the wingers, midfielders, and striker find enough space or make solid runs up the field, the forward will distribute the ball to players with more speed. Forwards use short and quick passes with movement off the ball to create openings for their team.

Most importantly, they are judged on their ability to score. Although they tend to obtain more assists than a striker, they are still expected to contribute many goals each season. Their size helps them score with their feet—and especially their head. Heading the ball with power and accuracy is a must because of how tall they are, compared to most other players on the field.

Forwards tend to fall into at least one of two categories: (1) clinical finishers, and/or (2) targets. Clinical finishers specialize in skills related to shooting with power from a distance. They are called "clinical" because they score on a high percentage of their shots and rarely hesitate to take an open shot. Clinical finishers can be recognized by the precise placement of their shots, as well as their high goals-to-shots ratio. The other type of forward is the "target," who receives the ball up the field and is great at distributing to faster teammates.

This player serves as an outlet for the midfielders and defenders, who can hold the ball up to wait for support. Furthermore, targets can make runs to create enough space and open the field for other players, thereby allowing their teammates to dribble past fewer opposing players to score.

However, let us not forget that a forward's major role is to put goals in the net, and their performances are judged by results. Although they may help pressure the other team to create turnovers, they still need to score to be considered productive.

Skills Needed:

- Judging a ball while it is travelling in the air to control or head it
- Good movement to evade the opposition's center backs and create space
- Powerful, accurate headers
- Formidable size
- Accurate, powerful strikes
- Good passing skills
- Can win physical battles with defenders

Advantages:

- Minimal defensive responsibilities

- Their large physical presence commands respect from the other team's players
- Usually gets the glory when their team wins because they were involved in scoring

Disadvantages:

- Takes responsibility when the team cannot score
- May be benched—or even cut—if they experience an extended period without scoring
- Often covered by two defenders from the other team

Example Players:

Abby Wambach - Washington Freedom and the United States Women's National Team. Wambach is known for her goal-scoring ability. She was not the fastest or best on the ball, but she was physical and had a very direct style of play. Additionally, her stellar positioning allowed her to get onto the end of long balls and crosses. Her 5'11" physique allowed her to excel in the air. In her international career, Wambach scored 184 goals in 256 international matches. 77 of those goals were scored with her head. She is the leading all-time international scorer between both men and women.

In her freshman year with the University of Florida Gators, Abby led her team to their first NCAA National

Championship over the 15-time champion North Carolina Tar Heels. Abby Wambach helped the Gators secure multiple titles. At the University of Florida, Wambach set school career records for goals, assists, points, game-winning goals, and hat tricks. Due to her successes in college, the United States Women's National Team recruited her. Throughout her career, she scored 184 goals—36 more than Mia Hamm, the next closest player. She even had one game in which she scored five goals. Abby has won a record six U.S. Soccer Female Player of the Year Awards, two Olympic Gold medals, and a World Cup title.

"I've never scored a goal in my life without getting a pass from someone else."—Abby Wambach

Zlatan Ibrahimović – LA Galaxy, Manchester United, Paris Saint-Germain, AC Milan, Barcelona, Inter Milan, Juventus, Ajax, and the Swedish National Team. Zlatan was born in Sweden to a Bosnian father and a Croatian mother. Therefore, he could have played for any of those three countries on the international stage. He chose to play for Sweden since he was born and raised there. He has two black belts in Taekwondo, which explains many of his unusual ways of scoring, as well as his ability to kick his legs well over his head to strike the ball out of the air. His international career has seen him become Sweden's all-time leading scorer. Zlatan is such a huge national hero in Sweden that his name has been added to the Swedish Dictionary as a verb. The term "to Zlatan" means to dominate with extreme talent. With a bigger-than-life personality, Zlatan is known for his ability to score and his confidence.

Zlatan is a multiple-time Top Scorer, Player of the Year, and Footballer of the Year. He is a French, Spanish, Italian, and Dutch Champion, and he holds many cups in these countries. Even during a short stint in England, he produced an English League Cup, an English Super Cup, and a Europa League win. While Zlatan was playing for Manchester United, he was asked who he felt were the best strikers in the Premier League. He said, *"Sergio Agüero and Romelu Lukaku are the best strikers in the Premier League."* The reporter then asked Zlatan why he did not list himself, and Zlatan stated, *"Lions, they do not compare themselves to humans."* This type of bold self-confidence is often associated with forwards and strikers since these players are responsible for winning games via goals for their team.

YouTube: If you would like to see a video on the forward position, then consider watching the *Understand Soccer* YouTube video: *Soccer Forward Tactics*.

Chapter 13

Striker

Jersey Number: #9

Strikers are positioned in front of the forwards and are the players nearest the other team's goal. A striker's main job is to strike (i.e., score). Additionally, strikers tend to create many scoring chances for their teammates. Many players and coaches use the terms "striker" and "forward" interchangeably because their roles are similar.

The coaching staff may occasionally require one striker to play next to the last defender (often the sweeper) of the opposing team. Since most opposing coaches will have a center back or full back marking your team's striker, standing next to the sweeper means that there will be two defenders "marking" the striker. This will create significant gaps in the defense, thereby making it easier for teammates to score. Conversely, if the striker is the team's only chance of scoring, then the coach will often tell them to find enough space to receive the ball, which often means going back to the midfield, like a false nine.

Teammates will pass to the striker as often as possible. Given that a striker is normally a team's best goal-scorer, the other team will apply significant pressure to them. Therefore, a striker should be fast enough to collect long balls played by both midfielders and defenders, a forward who will stand with their back to the net and collect the soccer ball like a Target. Strikers should read the defense to find holes in which to receive passes and score tap-ins. Strikers should have a powerful and accurate shot to finish from anywhere in or around the 18-yard box. Furthermore, strikers need to dribble to avoid the outstretched defender's legs.

Strikers often make great counterattackers. Counterattackers are occasionally midfielders but mostly strikers, who use their speed to move the ball quickly up the field. A counterattack occurs when the soccer ball is dispossessed from the other team and is played either towards the counterattacking player or into space ahead of the counterattacking player. Since the other team is in an offensive shape when they have the ball, they are not yet set to defend correctly after losing possession of it. Counterattackers take advantage of the few seconds in which the other team is working to get into their correct defensive positions. Great shooting abilities will make counterattacking even easier.

Lastly, strikers may also contribute defensively by stealing the ball from defenders. When the other team's defense has the ball, strikers should strategically pressure the less skilled defenders, or the defenders with poor positioning, to increase their chance of winning back the ball. Excitingly, if the striker can steal the ball from a defender, then they will not have to beat very many players on the other team to score.

Skills Needed:

- Powerful, accurate shots
- Fast reaction time to recover rebounds
- Speed and agility
- Can dribble the ball and beat a defender
- Can control difficult passes
- Can score

Advantages:

- Receives praise often for wins because they are the ones to score
- Often, they are the player who is most looked up to by fans
- Can dribble, shoot, and score, which makes them the envy of most other players

Disadvantages:

- Takes responsibility when the team cannot score
- May be benched—or even cut—if they have an extended period without scoring
- Often covered by two defenders from the other team

Example Players:

Sergio Agüero - Manchester City, Atlético Madrid, and the Argentinian National Team. Agüero is widely known as "'Kun" because of his resemblance to a character in a Japanese cartoon show called "Kum-Kum the Little Caveman," which he watched and enjoyed as a child. He made a name for himself at a young age by winning the U-20 World Cup for Argentina. He helped Atlético Madrid earn a spot in the Champions League for the first time in 10 years when he played for them. Additionally, during his time at Manchester City, Agüero's last-minute goal at the end of the 2012 season won the Premier League title for Manchester City after a 44-year drought. Agüero is an EPL top scorer, English Champion, Olympian, FA Community Shield Holder, and Europa League winner.

"You have to know your limits, so you know how to push past them."—Sergio Agüero

Robert Lewandowski - Bayern Munich, Borussia Dortmund, and the Polish National Team. Lewandowski is a prolific scorer and rare find. To further understand the human body and increase his ability to train and gain strength, he obtained a bachelor's degree in Physical Education. On September 22, 2015, he broke four Guinness World Records as a Bayern Munich substitute in a game versus Wolfsburg by scoring five goals in nine minutes. Keep in mind that this is in the top German flight against a quality team. He has about 16 Top League Scorer titles and has won Footballer of the Year about 10 times. Lewandowski is a German and Polish Champion, a German and Polish Super Cup Winner, and the Captain of the Polish National Team.

"As a striker, you are playing against big defenders. They try to throw you around. I try to play in behind them, and I need power. I know that I have to go to the gym and train. I train all the time."—Robert Lewandowski

YouTube: If you would like to see a video on the striker position, then consider watching the *Understand Soccer* YouTube video: *Striker in Soccer*.

Attacking Summary

An attacking soccer player's main purpose is to score. Therefore, consider grabbing a copy of the *Understand Soccer* series book **Soccer Shooting & Finishing: A Step-by-Step Guide on How to Score**, to learn the various ways to strike a ball, how to win in 1v1s, 1v2s, 2v1s, and 2v2s, and how to increase your chances of scoring using easily remembered steps. Although there are various ways to shoot the ball, the most common shot is a driven shot, performed as follows:

1. Start diagonal to the ball.
2. Plant one foot away from the ball.
3. With the leg you are striking the ball with, keep your toe down and out, and your knee facing the net so that you can use the bone of your foot.
4. Follow through, land on your shooting foot, bring your back leg forward, and point your hips where you want to score.

Chapter 14

The Coach

Outfit: Suit or Tracksuit

The soccer coach is largely responsible for managing everyone and their expectations. A soccer coach reports upwards and downwards: upwards towards the owners and directors of the club and downwards towards the fans, staff, parents, and players. In professional leagues and national teams, the Head Coach is referred to as the "manager." In an amateur game (e.g., youth and college teams,) the term "coach" is used instead.

Being responsible for so many people requires good communication skills and the ability to balance many things at one time. Ultimately, for a coach, the best way to manage expectations and relationships with others is to win. At the end of the day, a coach is judged by their wins and losses. Therefore, the team's record will decide whether the coach will continue to have success at the club or will face their departure—potentially even before the season is done.

Coaches play a huge part in selecting the players on their team. Keep in mind that when they take their coaching position with a club, there are already many players on the team. The coach must then determine which ones they want to keep, and which ones they are willing to cut, loan, or sell. These actions require that expectations are managed to avoid reducing the team's feeling of security, while still removing any parts of the team that have significant room for improvement by bringing in quality players.

Furthermore, a coach determines the team's tactics that are used in a game, the formation on the pitch, and where each player lines up. Whether it be the Tiki-taka tactics used by Pep Guardiola, or the fluid changes in tactics implemented by Sir Alex Ferguson, a coach needs to determine what play style will work best for their team. They must consider what type of soccer players are on their team, what each player can handle, and the fitness levels of each athlete to determine which formation would be best.

Lastly, knowing where to play each player based on their skills and abilities will help the team work together as one unit to win many titles, trophies, and awards. If you are a coach who is looking for drills with specific coaching points to use in practices that will increase your players' skills, then grab a copy of the *Understand Soccer* series book, ***Soccer Drills: A Step-by-Step Guide on How to Coach the Perfect Practice***.

Skills Needed:

- Confident actions and tone of voice
- Leadership traits
- Willing to accept responsibility for losses and praise players for wins
- Determines which tactics best suit their team
- Understands what type of player best fits each position
- Can receive feedback well and does not get anxious before games or after losses
- Can manage the different players' personalities

Advantages:

- Responsible for all wins
- Significant influence with owners and directors
- Close to total control of players and staff
- Decides who sits and who plays, based on players' performance in previous games and efforts in practice

Disadvantages:

- Responsible for all losses
- Manages relationships and expectations of owners, directors, players, and staff
- Can be fired mid-season and without notice

Example Coaches:

Pep Guardiola - Manchester City, Bayern Munich, and Barcelona. As a former soccer player, Guardiola won 16 trophies with Barcelona during his playing career. Interestingly, he turned down Barcelona's first request to sign him. His enjoyable demeanor and wonderful tactics have allowed Pep to reach heights that few coaches have ever reached. Guardiola's first coaching success came with Barcelona, where he implemented his Tiki-taka style of play. Tiki-taka involves high probability/short passing. This helps the team keep possession of the ball and frustrate the opposition, who is given possession as little as 15% of the time. Invented by Johan Cruyff, Guardiola implemented it at Barcelona, using Xavi and Iniesta at the center of the scheme. Furthermore, Pep was the brains behind bringing Lionel Messi into a more central position, so he could get many more touches on the ball. In just five years at Barcelona, Guardiola won 14 major trophies that included four La Ligas, two Copa del Reys, two Spanish Super Cups, two Champions Leagues, two Super Cups, and two Club World Cups. This includes the highly coveted Treble in 2008-2009. Furthermore, Guardiola has won the World's Best Club Coach, Club World Cup, English League Cup, English Super Cup, and German Cup, and he became the Champion in Spain, Germany, and England.

"In soccer, the worst things are excuses. Excuses mean you cannot grow or move forward."—Pep Guardiola

Sir Alex Ferguson - Manchester United. Having won 24 trophies in 23 seasons, Alex Ferguson established himself as the most successful manager in English soccer history. After he won a treble for Manchester United, the queen knighted him. She was very appreciative for all his efforts to advance English soccer and bestowed this great honor upon him because of it. Unlike Pep Guardiola, who has a preferred play style, Sir Alex Ferguson is always willing to cut, add, move around, and refocus his team's tactics and formations. Similar to Pep Guardiola, Sir Alex Ferguson has several trophies and awards to his name. He was voted the World's Best Club Coach, and he won multiple Champions Leagues, English, and Scottish Championships, as well as Super Cups. He has won the Intercontinental Cup, FIFA Club World Cup, English FA Cup, English League Cup, and Scottish League Cup.

"For a player—and for any human being—there is nothing better than hearing, 'Well done.' Those are the two best words ever invented in sports. You don't need to use superlatives."—Sir Alex Ferguson

Coaching Summary

Coaches have a variety of roles in the organization, from selecting formations and game tactics to managing players' personalities and their parents. If you are interested in learning more about the coach's role, and its impact on the team, pick up a copy of the *Understand Soccer* series book, **Soccer Coaching: A Step-by-Step Guide on How to Lead Your Players, Manage Parents, and Select the Best Soccer Formation**. This book will help you learn what it takes to make players want to play for you, parents willing to work with you, and team positioning to fit your players' abilities. Here is an excerpt from the book about the 4-3-3 formation:

The 4-3-3 formation is all about maintaining possession and scoring many goals. Late in games, when a team is down by a goal or two, the coach will often change the formation to a 4-3-3 to increase the chance of producing a goal at the expense of giving up a midfield player because in most circumstances, the number of points that a team loses by does not matter. In the 4-3-3, the midfielders are located more centrally and work to clog the middle of the midfield and dispossess the other team. Once possession is won, the ball is played to the wingers and carried up the field's flanks.

The 4-3-3 uses two offensive wingers to either transport the ball up the flanks and cross it into the 18-yard

box or cut in and strike the ball, like an inverted winger. The 4-3-3 also has two common variations: the 4-2-3-1, and the 4-3-2-1. Unsurprisingly, the 4-3-3 has had a tremendous impact on Spanish soccer, due to the hotbed of soccer talent that Spain has become.

Afterword

You may have noticed from the image at the beginning of the book of all the possible positions that there was no chapter on the Inside Right or Inside Left positions. This was intentional because the modern game has basically eliminated these positions. Granted, there are some teams that will shift the forwards' play style to resemble some of the characteristics of the Inside Right or Inside Left. For example, Mohamed Salah of Liverpool and the Egyptian National Team is a right winger, who has minimal defensive responsibilities and is told to push towards the middle, similar to an Inside Right. This play style has also appeared at times while Cristiano Ronaldo and Karim Benzema were teammates at Real Madrid.

Therefore, the play style of an Inside Right or Inside Left is a blend of a winger and a forward. The W-M Formation, an early formation of many teams in soccer, heavily used the Inside Right and Inside Left, but it has been out of favor for nearly a century. However, it is important that you know what it is, in case someone ever mentions it.

Also, the tactics and formations used by a coach can change dramatically. Each position mentioned in this book may change a bit, based on the coach's style of play. A coach may even change the position of a player, or their team's formation during a game, so it is important to have some overlapping skills, and the knowledge of what is expected of each position.

This book is all about helping you determine where you fit best on a team, where each of your players should be positioned, and what skills are needed for you to perform in the position you have always wanted to play. This book was created to reveal the advantages and disadvantages of all the different positions. To fully develop the skills that each of the individual positions require, read the other technical books in the *Understand Soccer* series.

As a player or coach who wants to become better at playing or teaching soccer, remember that your ability to grow is often directly tied to the knowledge that you gain and implement. Consider reading the *Understand Soccer* series book, **Soccer Coaching; A Step-by-Step Guide on How to Lead Your Players, Manage Parents, and Select the Best Soccer Formation**. This book provides numerous examples of great formations to be used by coaches. The combination of knowledge found in *Soccer Positions* and *Soccer Coaching* details the abilities needed for each position, and where all the players should be appropriately placed in the team's formation.

As with anything in life, you will need to practice and experiment to find out what works best. Never stop growing and trying to better your understanding of the game. Remember that your ability on the field will grow in proportion to the knowledge you gain. Becoming a better coach or player cannot simply be done overnight by reading one book, so continue to improve your soccer education to make sure that you become the best player or coach you can be.

Soccer Coaching:

A Step-by-Step Guide on How to Lead Your Players, Manage Parents, and Select the Best Formation

Introduction

The overarching objective of this book is to improve the soccer IQ of coaches and trainers. This book details various coaching styles, as well as ways to earn the team's respect and motivate them to work hard. This book does not cover the technical aspects of soccer, such as how to pass the ball, shoot properly, or perform a foot skill. Other books in the *Understand Soccer* series cover these subjects and are also available on Amazon.com.

Although the book cover is black and white, the concepts within are not quite so black and white. Each individual player is different, and although one concept can be used for many players, **most guidelines are not effective for all players**. If you are constantly searching for the one thing that will change everything, then understand there often is no "silver bullet" that will allow everything else to fall perfectly into place. As the coach, you are the leader of the team and should therefore lead by example. The harder you work, the harder your team will work. There is no perfect way to coach, and it normally takes time to find the style that works best for you and motivates your players.

Finally, this book reveals the "Big 3" formations used by many coaches and explains other common variations to help you determine whether your current formation is best for your team or if another formation would produce better results. Choosing your formation can be the deciding factor that achieves success.

Additionally, this book has many bonus takeaways, including great ways to deal with parents, and how to overcome the occasional difficult player.

The format of the book is assembled into three sections:
1. Topics Unrelated to Practice
2. Topics Related to Practice
3. Formations

Section 1

Topics Unrelated to

Practice

Chapter 1

Determine Your Coaching Style

One of the most productive things you can do before the season even starts is determine what type of coach you want to be. Do you want to be fair and give everyone equal amounts of playing time? Is your main goal to win? Is your main goal to build your players' character, confidence, and soccer skills? Do you have a preferred formation/playstyle, or will you pick one based on your players' abilities?

Coaching styles are often broken down into three major categories:

1. How you handle your relationship with your players and their parents.
2. How you select your playstyle and team formations.
3. How you advance your players' technical skills.

The first section will focus on how to handle your relationship with your players and their parents. In the two sections that follow, how to approach practice and implement different playstyles and formations will be discussed. To advance your players' technical skills, I recommend using the *Understand Soccer* series books on shooting and finishing, dribbling and foot skills, passing and receiving, and defending.

Before we get into the advantages and disadvantages of different approaches that you can take with your players and their parents, first make sure that you have thought about the main goal for your team, and then communicate your expectations to your players and their parents at tryouts (if applicable) or at the beginning of the season. Depending on the type of team you coach, and the age group of your players, telling the parents your style of coaching may make it easier for them to understand what you expect of their children and whether your team is a good fit for their child.

Remember that certain players and/or parents may not relate to the main objective that you are trying to achieve, and they may seek other teams to play for instead. If this happens, it may feel like they are rejecting you and your style. In reality, you are merely setting expectations for everyone at the outset of the season so that when the going gets tough, everyone will have agreed on the main objective beforehand. It is much better if the players and parents are onboard with the aspirations you have set than if they seek to undermine you halfway through the season because they expected one thing, but you delivered another. **Therefore, setting your overarching coaching goal(s) at the beginning of the season will make most of your decisions easier because there will usually be an obvious way to correctly handle the situation, based on your goal(s).**

For example, let us consider that your coaching style prioritizes winning, and a parent of one of your players is complaining that their child does not receive enough playing time. In this situation, you can point back to the beginning of the season, when you clearly set your expectations for the team which meant that playing time would be based on wins, and there would not be equal playing time for each player. If the parent does not like your decision, then you can reply, "Although it can be frustrating and at times it may not seem like it is working out perfectly for all parties, we did agree on the goals, values, and expectations at the beginning of the season. I am simply continuing to coach in this fashion, as it would be unfair to the other parents, players, and myself to change our objectives and expectations halfway through the season." **Fortunately, setting these expectations at the beginning of the season will reduce the number of conversations like this.**

Instead, maybe your goal is to build your players' character. In this situation, if a penalty is awarded in favor of your team, but your player informs you that they were not fouled, then you can easily tell the referee that there should not have been a penalty kick awarded and to let the other team take a goal kick instead.

In conclusion, setting expectations early for players and parents will make your decisions much more black-and-white and will reduce the number of frustrating conversations you will have with yourself, your team, and their parents. Set expectations at the beginning of the season, so the players and parents will know where you stand. If opting out of your team is an option in your league, then clearly expressed and understood expectations will allow them to do so if their goals do not align with your objectives.

To help you further understand the parents' expectations and their level of involvement with their child's soccer pursuits, as well as how to discover your players' personalities at the beginning of the season, grab your two-page free printout at UnderstandSoccer.com/free-printout, which includes a ready-made parent questionnaire to hand out during your first team meeting.

YouTube: If you would like to see a video on how to pick your coaching style, then consider watching the *Understand Soccer* YouTube video: *How to Pick Your Soccer Coaching Philosophy*.

Chapter 2

Get Hyped!

As mentioned in the previous chapter, it is important to determine the type of relationship you intend to have with your players at the beginning of the season, so your expectations can be set early on. **One highly recommended suggestion—especially for younger players—is to be "hyped."** Being hyped means you are your players' biggest advocate, you reward good behavior, you are quick to show praise, and you offer only constructive criticism.

Something most coaches do not use enough is the high five. In a time when hugging a player or giving them a pat on the back can be considered inappropriate, a high five is the happy medium between a hug and no contact whatsoever. After a high five (i.e., physical contact), the brain releases four feel-good chemicals: endorphins, oxytocin, serotonin, and dopamine. In contrast, when a player is faced with criticism and disdain, the stress chemical called cortisol is released instead.

During the contact of a high five, dopamine in the player triggers the release of even more oxytocin than just praise alone. This creates a bond between the coach and the player, while also reinforcing good behavior and making the player much more receptive to feedback. Obviously, you need to be a coach first, but it often will not hurt to be a friend, too. Players play harder for coaches they like and respect.

Consider Jürgen Klopp, who has coached Borussia Dortmund and Liverpool. Whenever his team scores huge goals, he has been known to run onto the field to the goal-scorer to celebrate with the team. Keep in mind that he has been fined for this, so I do not recommend doing it, but it does provide a great example of how fully invested Klopp is in his team. His charismatic nature allows him to be the premier coach in any league because he realizes that positive physical contact and becoming hyped shows his players that they are unified in achieving their dreams. Showing how much he cares has earned his players' respect and resulted in him taking the club team Liverpool to back-to-back Champions League Finals, including a victory in the 2019 Finals.

In her book, *Mindset,* Carol S. Dweck, Ph.D. presents numerous studies in which thousands of children showed how to improve players' abilities over the course of a season. Dweck insists on **praising your players for their hard work—*not* their intelligence**. When a coach praises their players for their intelligence, the player will look to complete more easy tasks to show off that intelligence. Because you communicated that their intelligence is most important, they will shy away from harder tasks that move them outside their comfort zone. Instead, praise your players for their effort and hard work, and they will seek challenges that demonstrate their willingness to work hard and develop.

Finally, remember that using constant criticism will only make your players mentally criticize you. Using constant praise will ensure that no mental burdens will slow the development of your players' soccer abilities. However, it is not suggested that you provide no criticism at all. You are the coach, after all, and your job is to direct your players towards improvement. Therefore, if they are doing something wrong, then praising their mistake will not help them grow. Instead, positively redirect them and make sure that you give thoughtful feedback, so your players will trust you, agree with you, and immediately implement your advice into their game. A chapter later in this book reveals exactly how to do this.

Chapter 3

Top 10 Non-Technical Topics That Every Coach Should Teach

1. **Make sure your team practices using their opposite foot**, not so much that they are as good with it as their dominant foot, but so they can still be a threat if the defender gives them space to their opposite foot. A player who cannot shoot with their opposite foot is one of the easiest players to stop because a defender can cut off their path up the field to their dominant foot without worrying about the player shooting with their opposite foot. Plus, a player who can shoot and pass with both feet will receive a huge confidence boost!

2. **Work on your team's weaknesses until they are adequate, but make sure you emphasize and practice your team's strengths, too**. For example, consider the next image. This team is outstanding at shooting, good at defending and passing, okay at dribbling, and needs significant improvement on headers. In this case, the coach should consider their team's strengths and weaknesses. The coach should focus on improving their dribbling and headers to the minimum line. From there, the coach should emphasize their shooting abilities to maximize their strengths. Too many coaches try to focus on everything at once, so their team can become well-balanced. However, using this approach ensures that the team will

become "jacks of all trades and masters of none." Instead, emphasize your team's strengths by making game plans that highlight them and minimize their weaknesses by practicing their weaknesses just enough to ensure that your team is hugely successful.

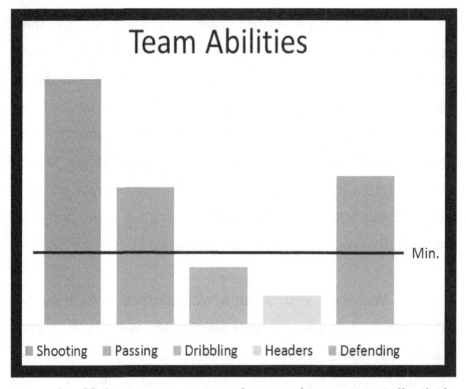

3. **Make sure your players know to tell their teammates where they want the ball to be passed using hand motions that are not visible to the defender.** They should not expect the pass that they want if they cannot tell the person who is passing the ball exactly where they want it. **Recommend that they point with their hands.** I suggest opening their hand in front of them if they want the ball at their feet, to the right if they want it slightly in front of them and to their right, or to the left if they want it slightly in front of them and

to the left. Similarly, if they want the ball played well in front of them, they should point to the spot on the field, so they can sprint to the ball and receive it in stride.

4. **Insist that your players demand the ball, not ask for the ball. They should yell for the ball, not call for the ball.** These shifts in wording (i.e., "demand" vs. "ask" and "yell" vs. "call") do a few excellent things for your players who want to receive a pass or be played a through ball. Demanding the ball and yelling for it with conviction will ensure that your players know their teammates want the ball and will do something productive when they receive it.

5. When a player's back is facing the direction in which they need to travel, they should look behind themselves just before receiving a pass from a teammate. This will allow them to turn with the ball quickly and confidently, which will help them score more goals and create more assists for your team. It cannot be stressed enough that your players should look over their shoulders when preparing to receive a pass. Depending on the situation, it may be best for them to just hold the ball and wait for support. A quick look will let them know where they should push the ball—or even if they should request a pass at all. **Encourage them to avoid twisting at the hips to look behind themselves because this takes too much time.** Instead, teach them to turn their head at the neck to take a swift look at the field, and the players behind them. If they have

space to attack, then they should yell for the ball and demand that it be passed to them.

6. **Remind your players not to worry about making mistakes**—especially during practices and scrimmages. Those are the times to make the mistakes, so your players can learn and develop their skills well enough to be used in a game. Remember that most people must learn from their own mistakes, so let them make mistakes in low-risk environments. Have your players encourage each other. Nothing discourages creativity and team chemistry more than teammates who criticize each other.

7. **Spend as much practice time as possible with a ball at your players' feet.** This will make them more confident with the ball. The best coaches who develop players are those who make each player in the system better—especially for 12-year-olds and younger. The more time you spend on tactics, the less time you can spend on the development of each player's skills. Focusing on team tactics is acceptable for high school, college, and pro-level teams. However, through the developmental ages, you should focus on each individual player, and their abilities with the ball. This will make them better players in any coach's system. Emphasize drills with lots of repetitions and lots of touches with the ball.

8. **Avoid placing blame on any individuals on your team.** It takes the whole team to win and the whole team to lose. Players will multiply the energy that you give them. If you yell at them, then they will build resentment and be afraid to make more mistakes, so their growth will come to a screeching halt. Usually, the player who made the mistake already knows the effect it will have on the team, so by drawing more attention to it, you are only shutting them down mentally in the near-term and giving their teammates an excuse for not working to overcome the error.

9. **Raise your expectations.** Players and students often perform to the expectations placed on them. A Harvard professor named Robert Rosenthal performed a study in which he told teachers that certain students in their classes had been tested and were determined to be highly intelligent. However, these students were all selected at random, and no student did anything to distinguish themselves from the others. For the next several months, the teachers treated these students differently. The students who were treated as smarter advanced quicker than the other kids in the class because their teachers had higher expectations of them.

10. **Give your players homework.** It can help double your players' touches. It is easiest to emphasize their touches with homework because it can be done with a soccer ball in any amount of space and teammates are not necessary. Working on

toe taps, foundations, shot fakes, fast footwork, and foot skills are easy to do. As your players age, they may have access to gyms, workout programs, and at-home DVDs to work on strength, flexibility, and speed, as well.

The Villarreal, Arsenal, and Paris Saint-Germain coach, Unai Emery, is best known for being a student of the game. He takes preparation very seriously by learning the best tactics for his players and assigning considerable amounts of homework. He gives his players USB drives with assignments on them. There was one particular player whom he feared was not taking the homework seriously, so he gave that player a blank USB drive. When Emery asked the player how his homework went, the player said it went well and was completed. Because there was nothing on the USB drive, the player was reprimanded for not doing the homework. Similar to how assigning homework helped Emery determine which players were dedicated, it too can help you determine levels of commitment and double your players' number of touches each week.

Bonus Tip: Arthur Skaer spent over five decades as a soccer player, and over two decades as a coach. He was voted Coach of the Year for Virginia's largest soccer organization. During each game he coaches, he makes one or two of his bench players record statistics of what is occurring on the field. Specifically, they record shots taken, completed passes, goal kicks, corner kicks, throw-ins, and goalkeeper saves.

Having one or two players record statistics while they are not on the field provides two major benefits: (1) The bench players will be much more engaged and will pay attention, which will further their learning of the game; and (2) You will get meaningful data from games to determine your team's progress and potentially uncover areas that need significant improvement. In addition to the statistics mentioned above, feel free to include additional metrics that you would like to track for your team.

If you are interested in learning more technical tips, consider picking up these four books in the *Understand Soccer* series: *Soccer Shooting & Finishing, Soccer Dribbling & Foot Skills, Soccer Passing & Receiving,* and *Soccer Defending.*

YouTube: If you would like to see a video on the top 10 non-technical ideas to teach, then consider watching the *Understand Soccer* YouTube video: *Soccer Coaching Points.*

Chapter 4

Clock Management

Soccer is a sport with a fixed amount of time. Unlike basketball and hockey, there are no timeouts in soccer. It is both a competition against the other team, and a race against the clock. Due to its set amount of time, managing the clock is essential. Often, games will have a scoreboard, so all players, coaches, and spectators will know roughly how much time is left. But it is at the referee's discretion to add time for game stoppages for injuries, discipline, and other unplanned stoppages of play. **If there is no scoreboard with the time, then a coach or two on your team should use their own watch to ensure that they correctly manage the remaining time.** Let us discuss a few ways to control the clock and prevent goals by the other team.

You should consider your team's playstyle, and the tactic you have chosen, but one of the worst things a team

can do is go purely into a defensive mode after scoring an early goal. The goal will have just generated momentum for your team and switching to a defensive mindset will limit your team's ability to provide a cushion of two or three goals. However, if your team has a great forward, and a solid defense, then you should absolutely look for opportunities to counterattack. Just avoid limiting your team's playstyle too early in the game.

The more you focus on defense early in a game, the more relaxed you will become. This will increase the chance of the opposing team closing the passing lanes down as your team's defense passes the ball and the other team may eventually intercept a pass in a position that can create a quick counterattack. **In short, playing very defensively too early in a game is a risk you should avoid.**

I have a good friend and teammate named Toni Sinistaj, who is always very ungenerous with restarts when his team is ahead. He does whatever he can to buy his team more time by taking longer to give the ball to the other team or making sure that his team is in position before giving the ball to the person who will take the throw-in. **He does a great job of avoiding placing his team in a disadvantaged position if he has the power to do something about it.**

I always give him a hard time for using this tactic anytime I am on the other team in a practice, scrimmage, or pickup game because I am trying to help my team win. However, I respect him and his strategy because it helps his team and is entirely within the rules. **However, remember that if you intend to use this strategy, your player must avoid taking too long because they may receive a yellow card from the referee for delaying the game.** This seemingly petty tactic might not be received well by the other team but remember that you are playing a competitive sport and using clock management strategies can be the difference between winning and losing a game.

By promptly giving the other team the ball during a game, you are letting them win a small battle. Do not retrieve the ball for the opposition because that will save them time and energy. Sure, allowing them to win these small battles will not often be detrimental to your team or lead to goals for the other team. However, a few times a season, these situations will turn into goals for the other team if they are paying better attention and are ready to act rapidly. **This is also an excellent opportunity for you to help your team catch their breath for a few seconds if they have been running nonstop.** Simply holding the ball for a bit longer or dropping it to the ground can buy your team some added physical and mental rest because the opposition must spend time collecting the ball.

If you are looking to kill time during a game, passing among the defenders and midfielders on your team is terrific. Granted, your team must have the talent to maintain possession. **If they do not, then in the last few minutes of the game, consider kicking the ball up the field or having one of your best players dribble the ball to the corner flag to prevent the other team from gaining possession.** Tactics like this may be considered a bit unsportsmanlike but are certainly within the rules of the game and should be considered when your team is looking for any advantage to run out the clock and win.

In summary, use appropriate clock management techniques when looking to sustain a lead in a game. Avoid quickly giving the ball to the other team when it goes out of bounds. Make them use their energy to fetch the ball and give yourself enough time to be properly positioned. Pass the ball extensively to tire the other team's forwards and midfielders, as they are the players who will need the most energy towards the end of the game to score. Finally, when in uncomfortable situations, kick the ball past the other team's defensive line or run the ball to the corner flag to delay the other team from gaining possession.

Chapter 5

How to Deal with Difficult Players

Often, coaches will have at least one difficult soccer player on their team. They may be productive on the field, but their attitude will hold them back—both on the team and in life. **From time to time, the idea of removing this player from your team may cross your mind, but it should only be considered after you have tried numerous ways to resolve the situation.**

To start, your mindset about the situation will make a big difference. The energy you give to it will affect your attitude and may lead you to fail at handling it. If you constantly think about how everything would be so much better if you did not have to deal with this player, then you may be looking at the situation with a narrow mind. Remember that you, as a coach, can use this situation to improve your communication abilities and conflict-resolution skills.

If you let yourself become emotionally drained by each situation that arises with the problem player, then you may become easily overwhelmed and miss the opportunity to learn. You can help a person with a difficult character trait, a person going through a difficult time, or a person who is stuck in frustrating circumstances. Remember that soccer is just one aspect of your players' lives, so not considering their whole situation will make it more difficult to resolve the problem.

Ideally, as a coach, you should not have to deal with this. However, choosing to be a person who helps a difficult player can give you a confidence boost that no winning season ever could. As best said by an ancient proverb, *"Ask not for a lighter burden but for broader shoulders."* **As a coach and fellow human being, do not stop trying.** Like most people, each individual on your team will respond in slightly different ways to criticism and positive reinforcement. They will deal with others and take responsibility differently.

Let us discuss several ways to improve the situation—or maybe even to completely resolve it. Consider the following when dealing with a difficult player:

1. Understand the real reason for their attitude.

2. Use positive reinforcement instead of criticism.

3. Increase their responsibility.

4. Do not forget about their parents.

5. Always keep your cool!

First, the most important thing to do when dealing with a difficult player is to understand why they are being difficult. Maybe their parents are going through a tough time. Maybe they have needs that are dissimilar to other kids their age. Maybe the player just really does not like you. Finding the root cause of their problematic behavior will significantly reduce the time it takes to understand how to best address the situation. Is there a certain scenario which provokes this behavior? Is the problem with another teammate? Is this a one-off situation that is totally out of character? Or has the player had similar difficult instances in the past? Use these questions and others to arrive at the root cause of their attitude.

Next, be a coach who is quick to reward the good. A coach who only points out mistakes and never congratulates their players when they perform well is difficult to play for over any significant period of time. This is why the legendary José Mourinho, coach of Porto, Chelsea, Inter Milan, Real Madrid, and Manchester United, tends to only last three years at each club. He uses criticism to shape his team during the first year to win a championship, then does okay in his second year, and is fired in his third year because his players become fed up with his criticism and do not want to hear it anymore. Only making negative comments about a player will only make them resent you and listen to very few of your suggestions.

If you have feedback that will significantly improve their game, then consider using a technique that is mentioned in the first book of the *Understand Soccer* series, *Soccer Training*. This is the "sandwich technique." First, compliment the player on something they are doing well. Keep the praise quick and straightforward, such as, "Good job approaching the ball diagonally when shooting." Then, give constructive feedback and explain why. For example, say, "If you plant your foot farther from the ball, it will allow you to turn your toe down and out more." Finally, end with another compliment, and an explanation, like, "Great job following through; it will ensure that you have plenty of power on your shot."

The sandwich method is crucial to help players who have a fixed mindset. By beginning with a compliment, you will break down any walls they have built up against constructive feedback. By ending with a compliment, you will leave them feeling like they are doing most things correctly. **By providing constructive feedback in the middle of two compliments, you will ensure that they hear your message and have positive associations with it.** Include explanations for all three points of feedback to ensure that the meaning of your message sticks with them, too.

Also, consider giving the difficult player more responsibility on the team. Ask them to take a leadership role, so they will have skin in the game. If you hesitate to give them leadership responsibilities because they have not showed that they can handle themselves, remember that this new role will likely uncover abilities and skills that they have never used before, as well as give them a sense of purpose and ownership over the outcome of each practice and game.

For example, you may have a player who is often talkative while you are explaining drills. Pull this player aside and mention that they have great communication skills, and because they can easily connect with the other players, you have a special role for them—"group supervisor during drills." Tell them that this role involves kindly asking any other player who is talking to please be quiet until the drill demonstration is over. **This newly created role will give them a sense of purpose and help ensure that they keep quiet themselves during your demonstrations.**

Furthermore, you can speed up the process of dealing with a difficult player by increasing communication with their parent(s). Communicate expectations, inform them of the progress being made, the areas that still need improvement, and ensure that they are on your side. This will make resolving the difficult player's behavioral problems much easier. **Remember that if a parent disagrees with you, then they will undermine all your suggestions and important feedback if they tell their child the opposite of your suggestions once they are in the car or back at their home.**

Finally, you must stay calm on the outside—even if this player's actions frustrate you on the inside. Showing signs of anger or irritation will subconsciously reveal that you are not very emotionally mature, either. When the player sees your reaction, they will be even less likely to listen to advice from you. A coach who yells and becomes angry easily is also one who loses their players' respect quickly. Temperamental coaches will have a hard time controlling the locker room for the duration of the season.

In conclusion, your mindset as a coach will make dealing with a problematic player either much easier or significantly harder, depending on how you perceive the situation. Your coaching time is limited, so use it wisely to determine the root of the problematic player's behavioral issues. Use positive reinforcement to create change, while potentially increasing their role on the team. Understand that having their parents onboard with your plan will make handling the problem/opportunity a lot easier and will allow you to keep calm throughout the process. Finally, remember that you are the adult here, so make sure that you act like it. It is important to avoid the mindset trap of thinking, "It is my way or the highway."

Chapter 6

How to Deal with Difficult Parents

Every parent is different, so things may work for certain parents and not for others. However, the worst thing you can do is attempt one or two things, realize that they do not work, and then assume that the parent is crazy, that nothing will work for them, and/or that nothing you do will ever be good enough. Remember, developing your abilities as a coach is a process when it comes to both team and parent management.

As a coach, sometimes, you must deal with unruly parents. Many of us have had parents who thought their child was an absolute all-star. However, we as coaches know that they probably should not have even come off the bench, based on their subpar skills and performances. That said, those parents will be personally offended if you do not play their child as much as they think is appropriate. **When this happens, one of the worst things you can do is tell them that their kid is not good.**

One tactic that is constantly taught to salespeople is to agree with people—even when you may not really agree with their point of view. To the other person, their opinion is reasonable, and you will benefit tremendously by acknowledging it. You may be thinking that you are not a salesperson because you are a coach. However, you are always selling your abilities as a coach to parents. You are always proving your worth to the club directors. You are always selling your team tactics and techniques to your players. Therefore, although you are not a salesperson in the traditional sense of selling a product, you are still selling your leadership to the players and parents. You are still selling your belief in the greater good to all parties involved.

Therefore, beginning your conversation with a parent by immediately disagreeing with them is the equivalent of digging yourself into a hole. The trick is to be gentle and explain that, as a coach, you are trying to get the team to work together as efficiently as possible. Mention that their child's performance has been lackluster in practices, and that you reward effort in practices with playing time in games. **This statement does multiple things: (1) It lets the parent know that their kid will play if they improve and show more effort; (2) It gently lets them know that their child has room for improvement**, which will make it easier to see the need for additional training, courses, and books on how to help their child improve in soccer; and (3) **It helps you not appear to be the enemy** and conveys that you want the best result for the team.

If a parent dislikes you, and they have influence with the other parents, then you could develop a problem wherein many parents are against you, which may destroy the team's chemistry. Remind yourself that they are just parents letting you know they are distraught, and they feel that something is wrong and should be improved going forward. Be open to their feedback. Do not see them as the enemy. See their opinions as opportunities to grow. Improve your communication and learn from other people's perspectives because when you watch the game, you only have one set of eyes to view the action. While you are standing on the sideline, the parents may see additional things from the stands that you cannot fully view. If they bring their perspectives to you, then say, **"Thank you for the feedback,"** and let them know that you will surely consider what they said. This will ensure that they are on your side and looking out for your best interest, too. Keep the communication lines open, so they will continue to want their child on your team, and so that the team's dynamic will not be disrupted by parents who are distraught by their child's playtime, position, etc.

Above all, remember that this is still your team. You are the coach, and you may make some mistakes. Perhaps you played someone in an incorrect position, instead of one that would have been better for the team, but it was not apparent to you at the time. You are only human, and mistakes can happen. The best way to overcome mistakes is to learn and grow from them to limit their chances of happening again.

Section 2
Topics Related to Practice

Chapter 7

Deliberate Practice

Deliberate Practice > Purposeful Practice > Habitual Practice

If you have read the *Understand Soccer* series book, *Soccer Parenting*, this chapter will look similar to the chapter on deliberate practice in that book. However, because this book is for the coach, who is conducting the team's training sessions, this chapter will describe the coach's role in ensuring that their players practice deliberately. **As a coach, it is important that you do not practice just "to get touches."**

There are certain hot spots around the world that produce outstanding performers. Consider country singers from Tennessee, hockey players from Canada, and soccer players from Brazil (more on Brazilian soccer players later in this chapter). These hot beds for talent have training programs that involve deliberate practice.

Deliberate practice is systematic. Regular/habitual practice often means dribbling, shooting, and passing in ways that you have done before and are comfortable performing. **Deliberate practice requires attention and is conducted with the specific goal of improving performance by learning**

where the practice needs to go, and how to get there, step by step.

Habitual/regular practice (e.g., trying to juggle) is not as good as purposeful practice (e.g., setting a specific goal, such as juggling the ball 30 times in a row). **Purposeful practice is not as productive as deep/deliberate practice.** Deliberate practice is purposeful practice with the added information and knowledge to understand how to find your weak areas, and how to improve them to advance quickly by progressively focusing on the areas just outside your comfort zone (e.g., juggling 30 times in a row using the part of your feet nearest the tops of the toes to become better at settling the ball out of the air with an instinctual first touch).

When you first start playing soccer, everything is new, and just going through the reps will be a new experience in which considerable learning will occur. **But training in something you are good at doing with no meaningful plan to progress can result in overlooking small errors and missing opportunities to improve.**

Mindless activity is the enemy of deliberate practice. The danger of practicing the same thing again and again without focusing on making small improvements is believing you are becoming better because you are working on your soccer abilities. In reality, you are likely only reinforcing habits that still have room for improvement, thereby wasting valuable practice time. The natural tendency of the brain is to turn repeated actions into habits. **Deliberate practice breaks down the overall process into components, thereby allowing you to identify your weaknesses, work on different ways to improve them, and bring all the training together for significant improvement.**

As a soccer trainer, one of the biggest areas I see trainees struggle with—especially at a young age—is shooting a driven shot with the correct form. To succeed, a trainee must start diagonal to the ball, then plant a foot away from the ball. With the foot that the player is striking the ball with, they must have their toe down and out, with their knee facing the target, so they can use the bone of their foot. Afterwards, they must follow through, land on their shooting foot, bring their back leg forward, and point their hips in the direction they want to score. This is a lot for a child or adult to learn if this is the first time they are working through the steps.

Therefore, instead of working on all the steps at once, it is best to start the trainee planted about a foot away from the ball and focus on striking the ball with the bone of their foot. After 10-15 repetitions of becoming comfortable striking with the bone of their foot, I will then have them work on taking a step to correctly plant next to the ball and continue to strike with the bone of their foot. Then, after 10-15 repetitions of this step, I have them take a step to plant next to the ball, strike the ball with the bone of their foot, and then work on following through to land past the ball. **The process is like building blocks; they add in one additional step until they are comfortable enough to add another, until they are comfortable enough with all the steps to shoot driven shots with the correct form.**

From earlier in this chapter, you may be wondering how Brazil has so many well-developed soccer players. Well, the most popular form of soccer in Brazil is referred to as *"futebol de salão."* This is 5v5 soccer and is often played on a basketball court. During a game, each player has six times more touches than they would in an 11v11 soccer game. The professor of soccer at the University of São Paulo, Emilio Miranda, says it is Brazil's "laboratory of improvisation." **Taking many more touches with little room/time to make decisions will force players to improve their pattern recognition learn how to act in many soccer situations.**

When developing soccer skills, you should emphasize lots of repetitions and quick feedback. **To implement this methodology into your coaching style, make sure that multiple players have balls at their feet during drills, and instead of 11v11 scrimmages or 8v8 scrimmages, focus on 3v3 or 2v2 scrimmages to ensure that more of your players are touching the ball at once.**

In the next chapter, *"Example of a Great One-Hour Practice,"* the example practice starts with fast footwork, in which every player has a ball at their feet, followed by dribbling and shooting drills, in which each player continues to obtain many touches of the ball. To ensure quick feedback, after showing the example of each of the skills, stand at the jab step (i.e., body feint, as shown in the image) for the first lap and tell your players how they can improve their skill for the first set of four laps. During the next set of four laps, stand at the shot fake and instruct each soccer player in how they can perform that skill more efficiently. During the last set of four laps, stand at the self-pass and inform your players how they can perform that skill better. This drill will ensure that there are numerous repetitions and immediate feedback.

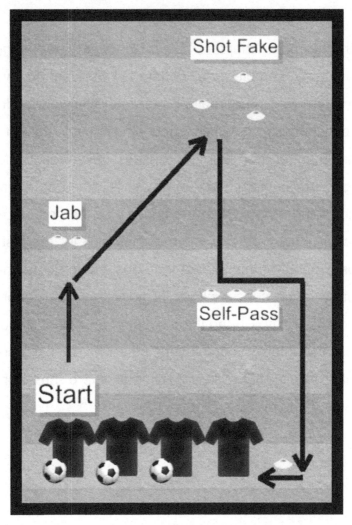

As a coach, it is important to understand the concept of deliberate practice to help your players advance their skills quickly and productively. If you are interested in learning more about deliberate practice, then consider picking up a copy of the book *Talent is Overrated* by **Geoff Colvin**. In the book, Colvin describes how Benjamin Franklin used deliberate practice to improve his writing skills, and Mozart used deliberate practice to become one of the greatest musicians of all time at a young age. He confirms the old saying that it takes about 10 years of deliberate practice to become an overnight sensation. Also, you may have heard others reference deliberate practice as the "10,000-Hour Rule," which states that it takes approximately 10,000 hours of deliberate practice to become great at anything.

YouTube: If you would like to see a video on coaching a deliberate practice, then consider watching the *Understand Soccer* YouTube video: *Deliberate Practice Soccer*.

Chapter 8

Example of a Great One-Hour Practice

Fast Footwork Warm-Up (10 mins)

Perform the following exercises between two cones set up 15 yards apart. Ideally, there should be two cones 15 yards apart for each player, so each player can experience as many touches as possible.

1. <u>Small Dribbles</u> – Toe Down and In – Right Foot, Then Left Foot
2. <u>Speed Dribbles</u> (i.e., Touches Every Step) – Toe Down and In Using Laces – Right Foot, Then Left Foot
3. <u>Dribbles at Speed</u> (i.e., One Big Touch) – Toe Down and In Using Laces – Right Foot, Then Left Foot
4. <u>Out-and-Ins</u> (i.e., 45° Touches Using the Inside and Laces of the Foot with Body Facing Forward) – Right Foot, Then Left Foot
5. <u>Push-Up Stop-Bottom</u> (i.e., Up-Stop) – Both Feet
6. <u>Self-Passes</u> – Both Feet
7. <u>Step-On-Step-Outs</u> – Both Feet
8. <u>Step-On-Step-Outs with a Shot Fake</u> – Both Feet

If some of these fast footwork items seem unclear, then consider subscribing to the *Understand Soccer* YouTube

Channel and watching the video: "_Soccer Dribbling Drills for Beginners_" to ensure that you understand how to perform each skill, as well as teach them. Additionally, a printable summary of this entire chapter is included in the free two-page printout at UnderstandSoccer.com/free-printout.

Dynamic Stretching (5 mins)

1. Leg Swings - 5 Forward and Back, 5 Right-to-Left (Perform with Both Legs)

2. 5 Jumps from Each Leg (Pretend You Are Heading a Ball)

3. While Walking, Pull Your Knee into Your Chest (5 Each Leg)

Dribbling Drill (20 mins)

The following drill is an excerpt from the _Understand Soccer_ series book, _Soccer Dribbling & Foot Skills_. This is a great drill using 9-10 cones for about 5-6 players. If you have more players, then I recommend making multiple courses of this drill and dividing the group up amongst each course of cones.

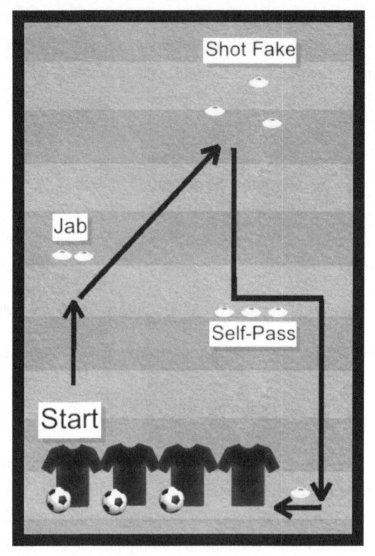

- Set up each of the skills roughly five yards apart.

- Attack the two cones and perform a left-footed jab step.

- Accelerate to the shot fake (i.e., the three cones in a triangle).

- Perform a right-footed chop shot fake.

- Accelerate with one push from your right foot to the three cones.

- Do a self-pass/la croqueta by passing the ball from your right foot to your left foot.

- Accelerate to the final cone and use a right-footed chop cut just past the cone.
- Finally, accelerate back to the start.

Note: Use only one push to accelerate to the next set of cones. Dribble with your head slightly up, not looking straight down at the ball. Make your shot fake look believable. This drill can be easily reversed to work on your skills in the opposite direction. Aim to have the players work to beat a specific time over three or four laps. Between sets, praise the players for what they did well and give constructive feedback on their mistakes.

Shooting and Finishing Drill (20 mins)

The following drill is great for an entire team. Forming two starting lines makes it so there are twice as many shots being taken. Twice as many shots means quicker improvement for the players who are going through the course, as well as great advancement for the goalkeeper, whose reaction time will be tested.

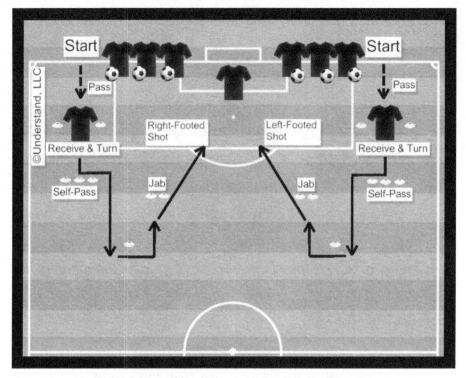

- Begin at the "Start" and pass to a player eight yards away.

- The receiving player should turn and attack the three cones.

- Do a self-pass/la croqueta from your right foot to your left foot (or vice versa.)

- Accelerate to the next singe cone and use a chop turn just past the cone.

- Attack the final two cones and perform a right/left-footed jab step.

- Take a big push past the cones and accelerate to the ball.

- Remember, the left side shoots right-footed, and the right side shoots left-footed.

- Players should switch lines after they shoot.

Note: Your players should use only one push to accelerate to the next set of cones. Players should dribble with their heads slightly up, not looking straight down at the ball. Make sure that the person who is receiving the ball is yelling and demanding the ball. Aim to make the players work to score a certain number of goals in a specific time (or over three laps.) Between sets, praise the players for what they did well and constructively correct any mistakes.

As you can see, this is great technical practice. It requires quick 30-second water breaks to ensure that everything is completed on time. **I recommend setting up the next drill before the previous one is completed if you have enough space and cones to do this.** Otherwise, just set up enough of the drill to demonstrate what needs to be done, then have your players start and quickly set up the rest of the drill. Planning predetermined practices to focus on the necessary areas for improvement will ensure that all your training time is used wisely.

If you are looking for drills with specific coaching points to use in practices that will increase your player's skills, then grab a copy of the *Understand Soccer* series book, *Soccer Drills*. You can also download the free two-page summary, which includes a print-ready version of this one-hour practice at:

UnderstandSoccer.com/free-printout

Chapter 9

Rondos

There are hundreds of different things that coaches can focus on with their team during practices. However, the trick is to apply the 80/20 principle when determining what a practice should include. Specifically, the 80/20 principle states that 80% of your beneficial coaching results will come from only 20% of the things that you teach to/work on with your team. This concept is further discussed in the *Understand Soccer* series book, *Soccer Mindset*.

With the 80/20 principle in mind, a key part of an optimized team practice that gives outsized benefits is the "Rondo." A Rondo is a training game similar to "Keep-Away," wherein one group of players must maintain possession of the ball by passing it around players on the opposing side. This game can be played with as little as three players, and there is no maximum number of players. **Rondos train your team to work together, pass in tight spaces, avoid holding onto the ball for too long, and make decisions quickly.**

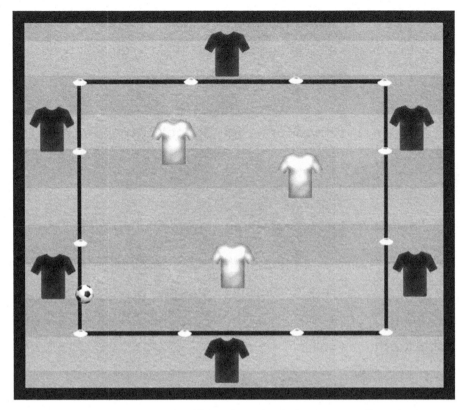

The following are recommendations when using the Rondo:

- **Fewer players are often better.** Form multiple groups of Rondos simultaneously so that more players will be in possession of the ball and improving their skills. An 11v11 Rondo will not help your players as much as a 6v3 Rondo.

- **Create a small area for the Rondo to take place in.** The key target with a Rondo is to make your team more comfortable with playing the ball when they are pressured and decreasing their reaction time for decision-making.

- **Make the Rondo age-specific.** Having a super-complex Rondo, or one in which the players must play one-touch, will not be helpful for a team of seven-year-olds. Conversely, allowing many touches in a huge space will not make high school soccer players much better, either.

Example Rondo for a High School Soccer Team:

- 15-yard x 15-yard box

- Six players on the outside, three players on the inside

- When the players in the middle obtain possession of the ball, the person who made the mistake, and the player to their right and left, will enter the inside of the square. The three players inside the square will join the outside.

Rondo Coaching Tips:

- As your team becomes better at Rondos, you can make the box smaller or limit the number of touches to two or one. This will improve their passing and receiving skills. The Rondo relates to most game situations (except for shooting.) This will result in a game-like training session for your team.
- To teach transitioning from offense to defense after possession is lost, you can go from allowing the players on the inside to walk to their positions on the outside of the square to a more game-like approach, wherein the players must immediately transition when possession changes. This will force

players to develop their transitional awareness and mindset, which will in turn keep them from being caught off-guard.

- Create triangle shapes and teach your players how to move so that the player passing the ball will always have two teammates open as targets.

In conclusion, the Rondo is a must for every coach and can even be a terrific warm-up for players to engage in prior to the start of a game. Rondos are used by many powerhouse clubs, such as Liverpool, Barcelona, Ajax, Bayern Munich, and Manchester City. Even the Dutch player and former coach of Barcelona, Johan Cruyff, said, *"Everything that goes on in a match—except shooting—you can do in a rondo. The competitive aspect, fighting to make space, what to do when in possession, and what to do when you have not got the ball, how to play one-touch soccer, how to counteract tight marking, and how to win the ball back."*

YouTube: If you would like to see a video on coaching a rondo, then consider watching the *Understand Soccer* YouTube video: *Rondo Coaching*.

Chapter 10

Ajax Training Method

In international club soccer, the biggest non-national teams play each other over the course of a season and in tournaments to determine the best teams in the world. Examples of club teams are Real Madrid, Paris Saint-Germain, Manchester United, Juventus, River Plate, Bayern Munich, etc.

Clubs have two traditional ways of obtaining good players: (1) The clubs listed in the previous paragraph tend to purchase their players for large sums of money; (2) The other type of club takes young talent and trains them to become the world's top performers. Often, the trained players become so good that the club sells them for large sums of money to teams that are willing to pay.

One of the best examples of a club falling into the latter category is Ajax, a team from the Netherlands. This club is constantly advancing in international competitions because of their educational programs for young athletes, *not* by purchasing superstar players. This speaks volumes about their training methodologies. A few of the top names from within their ranks who have trained from a young age are Johan Cruyff, Christian Eriksen, Wesley Sneijder, and Dennis Bergkamp. Zlatan Ibrahimović and Luis Suárez also played for Ajax.

One of the biggest underlying decisions that impacts their training is their focus on age-specific soccer skills. Players who are 12 years old and younger focus mostly on their technique with the ball. This means they are working on shooting and finishing, passing and receiving with proper form, heading the ball, and learning various foot skills and the best forms of dribbling. The logic behind this is that these players will play in many systems over the course of their career. Therefore, it is best to focus on building the player, so they can easily adapt to any coaching system. This style of training ensures that they take more touches with the ball than nearly all other players their age. More deliberate touches will quickly raise their confidence, thereby allowing them to become effective soccer players who can play on the game's biggest stages.

For players between the ages of 12 years old and 15 years old, the club directs their attention towards working as a team and being comfortable with building a play by passing the ball. Granted, this does not mean that 12-year-olds and younger players never pass the ball, nor does it mean that the 12-15-year-old players never focus on shooting and foot skills. It merely places the emphasis on one or the other during practices, without entirely cutting out the other important areas of soccer.

Finally, 15-year-olds and older players change their focus to the tactical progression of the team's playstyle. This age group focuses on where each player fits into the team's overarching theme. Ajax has found this to be an appropriate time to increase their strength training, as well.

As a whole, this is a sound system for a club. Granted, you may coach only one age group. But pushing to prioritize certain types of training over different periods of a soccer player's career will turn your club into a premier organization that players seek to join. Yes, this will take coordination with club directors and other coaches, but it is important to understand. Focusing only on foot skills with 18-year-olds and focusing only on team tactics with eight-year-olds makes little sense. Therefore, the appropriate training for each player will be highly impacted by their age.

YouTube: If you would like to see a video on the Ajax Training Method, then consider watching the *Understand Soccer* YouTube video: *Ajax Training Method*.

Chapter 11

The Six-Second Defense

There are two phases of defense: (1) the transition to defense, and (2) being on the defense. According to professional football coach and former player Pep Guardiola, one of the most successful coaches in the world, **Recoveries during the transition to defense are crucial because the best time to regain possession is within the six seconds after the ball was stolen**. Recovering the ball with a six-second burst of high-intensity pressing is also known as "Gegenpressing" or "counter-pressing."

Often, a turnover by your team occurs in the other team's half, so the press is performed by the forwards and midfielders. When forwards and midfielders press the other team for the ball, it is considered to be "high-pressing" and doing it throughout the game will take considerable energy away from the forwards and midfielders who are responsible for scoring. This is why Pep Guardiola and Jürgen Klopp tell their players to counter-press for roughly six seconds, and then assume a standard defensive formation that takes less energy. **This approach requires all the players nearest the ball to rush towards the individual in possession, while the rest of the team moves closer together in a tighter defensive formation.**

The close players shut down passing lanes and attempt to force an immediate mistake. If no error occurs, then the tight positioning is the basis for a tremendous defensive formation. Notice in the below images how the "O" team's defense becomes compacted towards the middle of the field when possession is lost, while ensuring that the opposing player "X" with the ball has no passing lanes open.

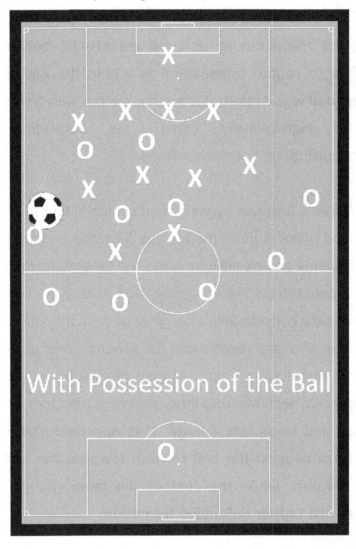

With Possession of the Ball

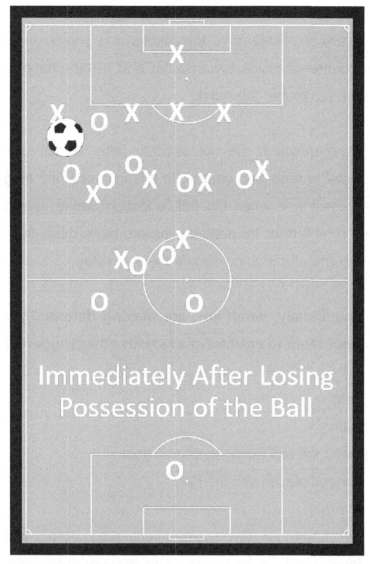

Immediately After Losing Possession of the Ball

For the six-second defense to be effective, each player must do their part. Pep Guardiola even sold the high-profile players Zlatan Ibrahimović and Yaya Touré because they did not want to be responsible for intense pressing. Counter-pressing is tiring when a loss of possession means the five players nearest the ball need to make 5-10-yard sprints to win the ball back and eliminate passing lanes. However, if this strategy is implemented at the beginning of the season, then your players will likely have the fitness and energy needed to handle counter-pressing towards the end of the season, when games tend to matter the most.

As mentioned, the six seconds after a ball is lost is instrumental in regaining control. In this instance, the trigger for counter-pressing is when the ball is lost. However, this can be coached a bit further for players who are more mentally mature and can comprehend and execute the team play.

Specifically, when you are playing defense, you can coach your team to counter-press with other triggers, like:

- Slow pass
- Bad touch
- Player with the ball facing their own goal
- Off-balanced player with the ball

But remember, this is only effective as a team tactic, so each player needs to know your team's triggers to overwhelm the opposing player with the ball, while providing your defensive players with enough time to regain their shape. This type of triggered pressing resulted in Germany winning the World Cup in 2014 and the German club team Bayern Munich winning the UEFA Champions League in 2013.

YouTube: If you would like to see a video on Gegenpressing, then consider watching the *Understand Soccer* YouTube video: *Counter Pressing - How to Coach the Six-Second Defense*.

Section 3
Formations

Chapter 12

4-4-2 Formation

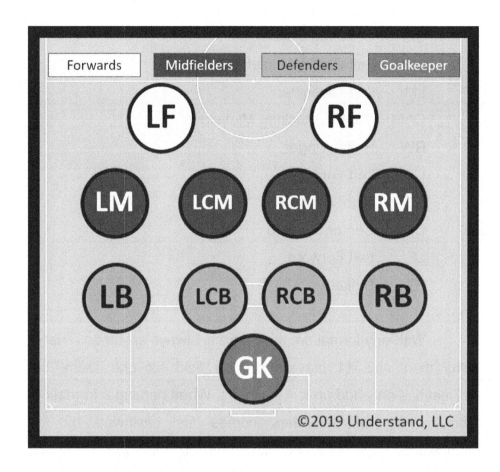

GK	Goalkeeper
RB	Right Back
RCB	Right Center Back
CB	Center Back
LCB	Left Center Back
LB	Left Back
RWB	Right Wing Back

LWB	Left Wing Back
CDM	Center Defensive Midfielder
RM	Right Midfielder
RCM	Right Center Midfielder
CM	Center Midfielder
LCM	Left Center Midfielder
LM	Left Midfielder
CAM	Center Attacking Midfielder
RW	Right Winger
LW	Left Winger
RF	Right Forward
CF	Center Forward
LF	Left Forward
ST	Striker

With any formation, the goalie is always assumed. That is why there are 11 players on the field for one team, but formations only add up to 10 players. When naming a formation, the number of defenders comes first, followed by the midfielders, and then the forwards. In this and upcoming chapters, the "Big 3" and most other formations will be discussed to help determine which formation is best for your team. **You will also learn that each formation is stronger against some formations and weaker against others**. However, a well-selected formation alone cannot compensate for a team that cannot pass, shoot with accuracy, has minimal skill with the ball, and does not defend properly. Dynamic players who can change as needed are best for any formation, but a well-selected formation with the players' abilities in mind will reap the biggest results. Therefore, a good coach should consider their team's skills and deficiencies when determining the best formation.

The standard formation for most youth teams with new coaches, and many professional-level English teams, is the 4-4-2 formation. Some club teams shy away from this formation because many top directors see this as a formation used by teams who are unconvinced of their players' abilities and their coaching staff's skills. This formation is easy to teach at any level and does not involve advanced offensive game planning.

This formation uses four defenders, four midfielders, and two forwards. **The most common variation of the 4-4-2 is where the four midfielders are in a diamond formation.** This formation has one center attacking midfielder, and one center defensive/holding midfielder. Also, you may find the forwards stacked, instead of side-by-side. The topmost forward would act as the striker, and the forward between the striker and center attacking midfielder would act as the center forward.

The other most common variation of this formation is the 4-1-3-2, which uses a holding/defensive center midfielder, and three other midfielders/wingers who play higher up the field.

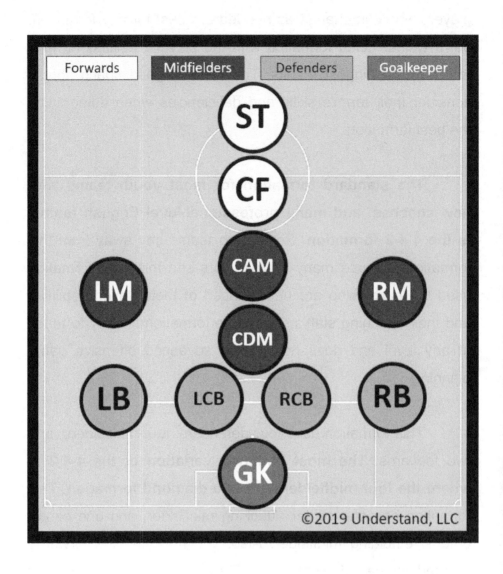

Forwards   Midfielders   Defenders   Goalkeeper

©2019 Understand, LLC

Strengths

This balanced formation provides enough players to attack and defend. This type of formation ensures that a team can easily work the ball from the defense to the midfield and (usually) maintain continuous possession. **Many coaches prefer this formation because it is the easiest to teach, and one of the simplest for players to understand.**

This formation is great when a team does not have many all-star-caliber players who can carry the scoring responsibilities by themselves. **Furthermore, this formation provides width in the midfield, and enough defense to slow the opposition's progress both up the flanks and the center of the field.** Conversely, the 4-4-2 is great for teams with outside midfielders or wing backs who excel at the crossing the ball into the box towards forwards/strikers, as well as midfielders who excel at scoring from crosses. This formation has an advantage in the midfield over teams playing a 4-3-3.

Weaknesses

This formation heavily relies on good forwards and strikers who can dribble past and possess the ball effectively against the opposing defenders. Teams who implement this formation often only score a couple of goals per game. This formation does not have enough forwards/strikers to overcome an opposing team using the 5-4-1.

Without proper coaching, the outside midfielders may act like wingers and not track back well enough on defense. **Conversely, the outside midfielder may be so concerned with marking the opposing player in their position that they focus more on defense than producing goals.** This type of player will spend their energy tracking back and making sure that their opponent never scores, but it will be the expense of creating scoring opportunities themselves. Finally, the 4-4-2 has been around for years, so it is predictable. Therefore, the other team will usually be familiar with ways to beat and defend against it.

Notable Teams That Have Used the 4-4-2 Formation

Arsenal's "Invincibles" team of 2003/04 achieved great success using the 4-4-2. This is the only English Premier League team in the modern era to go an entire 38-match season without losing a game.

The Manchester United team of 1998/99 used this formation to win the treble under Sir Alex Ferguson. Sir Alex Ferguson's soccer mind resulted in many variations of the 4-4-2 to confuse the opposition, but the general formation largely remained the same.

Chapter 13

5-4-1 Formation

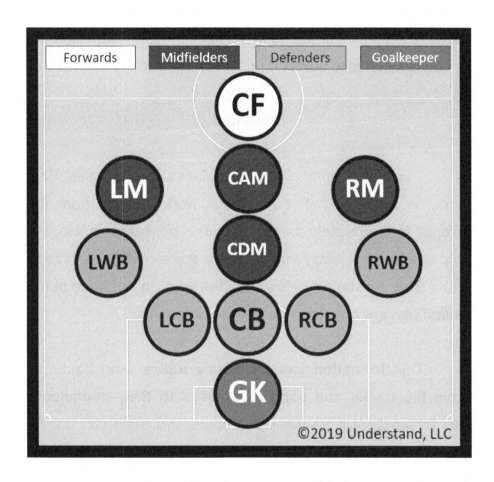

Forwards | Midfielders | Defenders | Goalkeeper

CF

LM CAM RM

CDM

LWB RWB

LCB CB RCB

GK

©2019 Understand, LLC

This formation features five defenders, four midfielders, and one forward. **The 5-4-1 is a very defensive formation.** 10 players out of the team's 11 will have defensive responsibilities, so this formation is for teams with a lot of defenders who care most about keeping the other team off the stat sheet. Often, teams with less skilled players will use this formation. Also, this formation is used by tiny nations who do not have the same scoring abilities as the world soccer powerhouses. Having many players behind the ball will ensure many 0-0 ties or 1-0 victories for the team. This formation is effective when playing more talented teams in a tournament, as the team can hope for penalty shootouts to advance in the tournament.

Strengths

The 5-4-1 emphasizes a defense-first mindset. This formation ensures that a team can work the ball from the defense to the midfield and still maintain possession. Also, the only way to consistently score against this formation is through errors. **This formation helps coaches who do not have many skilled players consistently scoring in games.**

This formation can effectively utilize wing backs to drive the flanks and send in crosses to their midfielders and forward. With so many defenders, this team can quickly counterattack the other team by booting the ball up the field and letting their dominant center forward go to work.

Finally, a 5-4-1 has a defensive advantage over teams that play a 4-4-2.

Weaknesses

This formation makes it difficult for the other team to score, but also **makes it difficult for your own team to score**. Most players will be too deep in defensive positions to create chances or support the lonely center forward while attacking. Also, because there is little opportunity for players on the team to score, this formation is often disliked by many midfielders and forwards because they want to score goals, and this formation does not cater to that.

This lack of goal production can quickly reduce the spirits of many midfielders and forwards, who may feel like they are not making a meaningful impact on the team. This formation requires teamwork and discipline because incorrect moves can open passing lanes and allow the other team to score. Also, this formation relies heavily on an all-star center forward, who can control the ball and score—even with multiple people covering them.

Finally, this formation does not have enough forwards/strikers to keep pace by scoring enough goals to keep up with a team using a 4-3-3.

Notable Teams That Have Used the 5-4-1 Formation

The Chelsea team of the 2004/05 season earned the most points in an English Premier League season up to that point in time. This team was coached by José Mourinho and featured Didier Drogba as a pivotal center forward. He was required to score and hold the ball for teammates. Without a great point-man, this formation is not as effective.

In the 2014 World Cup, the small island nation of Costa Rica won their group against the huge soccer nations of Uruguay, Italy, and England. Their manager, Jorge Pinto, realized his team lacked the skills and abilities of their opponents, so they wanted to "park the bus" in front of their net and counterattack when they dispossessed the other team. Costa Rica was knocked out of the quarterfinal by penalty kicks but only gave up one goal during their entire campaign.

Chapter 14

4-3-3 Formation

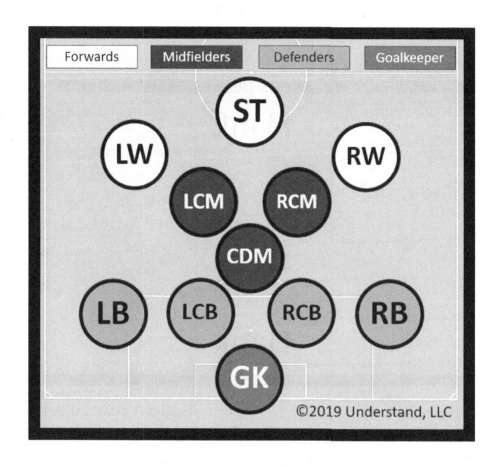

This formation features four defenders, three midfielders, and three forwards. **The 4-3-3 formation is all about maintaining possession and placing a strong emphasis on scoring many goals in each game.** Late in games, when a team is down by a goal or two, the coach will often change the formation to a 4-3-3 to increase the chance of producing a goal at the expense of giving up a midfield player. This is because, in most circumstances, it does not matter how many goals a team loses by. In the 4-3-3, the midfield is located more centrally and works to clog up the midfield and dispossess the other team. Once possession is won, the ball is played to the wings and carried up the field's flanks.

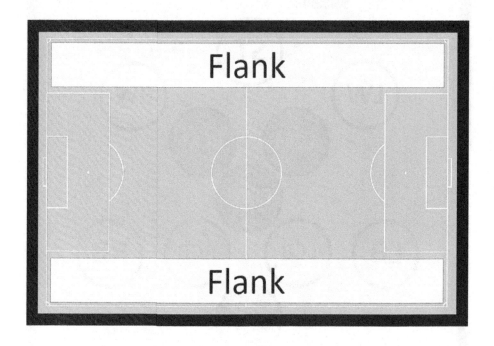

The 4-3-3 uses two offensive wingers to transport the ball up the flanks and cross it into the box or to cut in and strike it like an inverted winger.

The 4-3-3 formation has had a tremendous impact in Spanish soccer—to no one's surprise—because of the talent hotbed that Spain has become for soccer players. A common variation of the 4-3-3 is the 4-3-2-1.

If any these player positions seem a bit confusing, then consider grabbing a copy of the *Understand Soccer* series book, *Soccer Positions*, to fully understand each major position in soccer and the role, skills needed, and number associated with each position.

Strengths

The basic 4-3-3 formation is the ultimate attacking formation of the "Big 3." This formation often has a high defensive line in which the whole defense pushes up the field to be readily available if the other team obtains possession of the ball, as well as to use the offside trap against the opposing team. If you have two very fit wingers, then the 4-3-3 formation can become a 4-5-1 formation, based on the flow of the game—especially when possession is lost.

The 4-3-3 generally uses three central midfielders, who aim to dominate the center of the pitch and force the opposing team to move the ball up the sides of the field. This formation works best with technically strong players who can maintain possession of the ball. Furthermore, the positioning itself makes maintaining possession easier by featuring many passing angles and plenty of offensive players ready to receive the ball. Because the 4-3-3 has more forwards than the formations discussed in previous chapters, the three attacking players are expected to press the other team's defense when the opposing team has the ball. A defensive turnover by the other team will make it easy for the attackers to score because there will be few opposing players to beat. Also, because the flanks of the field are so open, the outside defensive backs will often function more like wing backs and carry the ball up the wings of the field. Finally, a 4-3-3 has an offensive player advantage over teams playing a 5-4-1.

Weaknesses

The 4-3-3 may be an unreasonable formation for a team that does not have three players who can consistently score. Using a 4-3-3 requires a team's forwards to work well together, and each offensive player must contribute in terms of goals and assists. Often, because this formation has many offensive players, one of the midfielders will need to play like a center defensive midfielder (i.e., holding midfielder) to help stop the other team from quickly moving the ball up the field after they gain possession of it.

Furthermore, having six players with some offensive responsibilities may result in situations where **the other team can counterattack** and quickly pass by six players seemingly at once. Because many midfielders will be centrally located, the wings/flanks of the field will often be wide-open and easy to carry the ball into.

The trick to a successful 4-3-3 formation occurs when the team using the 4-3-3 gains possession. Without the ball, the players should be compact, but when possession is gained, the entire team must work to spread out, both in terms of width and depth, across the field.

Additionally, the 4-3-3 formation provides many gaps, which an opposing team with good passing abilities can exploit to quickly move the ball from a defender to a midfielder, and then to a forward. **Conversely, because the team using the 4-3-3 tends to be compacted towards the middle of the field, the opposition can easily play the ball from one side of the field to the other. This will allow them to begin attacking from the opposite side of the field, which will have no wide players to prevent this from occurring.** Finally, this formation does not have enough midfielders when matched against a 4-4-2.

Notable Teams That Have Used the 4-3-3 Formation

The 2014/15 Barcelona team won the treble by winning La Liga, the Copa del Rey, and the Champions League titles. Barcelona effectively used this system under their coach, Luis Enrique, because they had the lineup of a generation. With Messi, Suarez, and Neymar as attacking players, and Rakitić, Sergio, and Roberto as the midfield, this team was formed with the sole purpose of moving the ball to the three attackers, known as "MSN." MSN netted 122 goals, the most in a season during all competitions for an offensive trio in Spanish soccer history.

The 2008-2012 Spanish national team implemented the 4-3-3 as a possession-oriented formation. They became known for their Tiki-taka style of passing (i.e., one-or-two-touch passing) to wear down opponents, so the other team would go for stretches of up to 10 minutes without even touching the ball. Forcing the other team to constantly play defense and chase the ball allowed the Spanish national team to win the Euro 2008, the 2010 World Cup, and the Euro 2012.

Chapter 15

Other Formations

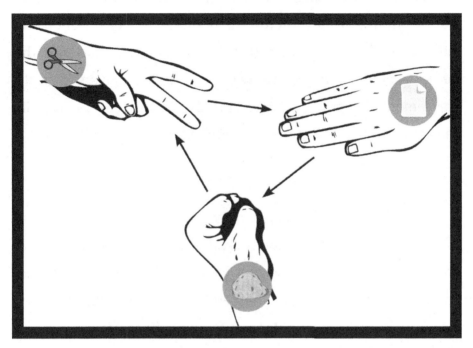

For the formations already mentioned, **think of the "Big 3" formations (e.g., 4-4-2, 5-4-1, and 4-3-3) as "Rock, Paper, Scissors."** Each formation has advantages over another and is disadvantaged by another. The 4-4-2 provides an advantage over the 4-3-3 because the 4-4-2's four midfielders can overwhelm the other team's three midfielders. The 4-3-3 provides an advantage over the 5-4-1 because having so many attacking players provides a constant barrage against a team that is very defensive-minded. The 5-4-1 provides a defensive advantage over the 4-4-2 because the attacking forces are often overwhelmed by the number of defending players.

A good coach will assess their players' skills and team's abilities against the opposing teams. **A knowledgeable coach will know that forcing a preferred formation on a team that cannot handle it is a recipe for disaster. A great coach will pick their formation based on their players, and not the other way around.** Teams with very skilled players typically have more forwards and favor the 4-3-3, whereas teams with less technical skills but more good defenders will benefit from a 5-4-1.

As we have discussed in the past few chapters, the 4-4-2, 5-4-1, and 4-3-3 are considered by many to be the "Big 3" formations. However, based on your team's skillset, a different formation may be better. The remaining formations are listed below, in order of most defensive to most offensive:

Most Defensive: 5-3-2

4-2-3-1 (like a 4-5-1)

3-2-3-2 (like a 3-5-2)

3-4-3

4-2-4

3-3-4

W-M (like a 3-2-5)

2-3-5

1-2-7

Most Offensive: Dutch Total Football

Note: *Please keep in mind that there are many variations of each of these. You may have heard of or read about some of them. Therefore, this order is not definite; it only acts as a guide to aid in selecting a formation for your team.*

5-3-2

The 5-3-2 is a defensive-oriented formation, like the 5-4-1. However, this formation adds another forward to help score. This formation often has three midfield players centrally located. The ball is typically moved up the center of the field. A variation of this formation involves a sweeper behind the line of four defenders. **This formation requires midfielders and forwards who are skilled at receiving the ball and using foot skills to beat defenders.** This formation is strong in the middle of the field but lacks the width needed in the flanks. Therefore, opposing teams will find many opportunities to cross the ball into the box from wide positions on the field. To counteract excessive amounts of crosses, often the rightmost and leftmost defenders will defend farther up the field and work the ball up the sides of the field to help the midfielders and forwards when their team has possession.

The Italian "catenaccio" is a defensive variation of this formation, with the innovation of using a sweeper (also known as a "libero" or "free man.") The four main defenders had the task of strictly man-marking the opposition's forwards in a time when the opposition likely had at least four forwards. The sweeper acted as a layer of additional defense when the other team had the ball.

4-2-3-1

The 4-2-3-1 is like a 4-5-1 in that there are two holding midfielders, and three midfielders who are focused primarily on helping the team score. **The holding midfielders can win the ball and significantly limit the other team's ability to move the ball through the middle of the field. A great holding midfielder can be a phenomenal passer with great accuracy and wonderful vision to pass to attacking midfielders, wingers, forwards, and strikers, who can in turn receive the ball and travel behind the opposition's back line.**

The 4-2-3-1 has many centrally located players. Therefore, one of its greatest weaknesses is its lack of width to help carry the ball up the sides of the pitch.

3-2-3-2

The 3-2-3-2 is like a 3-5-2 in that there are five midfielders. This formation (and the others discussed so far in this chapter) all lack width in the midfield. **Often, these** centrally oriented formations will be used by coaches with players who are talented with the ball at their feet (i.e., players with good foot skills, as well as passing and receiving abilities.) On one hand, staying centrally located makes it easier for the opposition to attack in the flanks. On the other hand, clogging up the middle ensures that opposing teams with very skilled players cannot effectively move the ball through the most dangerous part of the field, the middle.

3-4-3

The 3-4-3 is a favorite of many youth teams, including the Dutch powerhouse club, Ajax. As mentioned previously, the Ajax club team cares deeply about developing their talent from a young age. As such, they care more about focusing on each player's skills and abilities than on which formation the players use. Specifically, Ajax is not as concerned with wins and losses in their youth programs as they are with developing each player in the system.

Personally, this formation really resonates with me because having only three defenders will ensure many 1v1 situations against attacking players on the opposing team. This in turn greatly increases the abilities of the defenders, who are required to read the field from a young age and know when to dive in for the ball and when to slow the attacker and wait for support.

Next, having four midfielders and three forwards will help overwhelm the other team's defense. Having many players attacking means the offense will have more touches on the ball. More touches on the ball will ensure that players gain additional experience quicker. **Because there are usually not enough defenders on the opposing side to control the 3-4-3, the attacking players will become more comfortable working with their teammates and improving their 1v1 foot skills, and they will appreciate having more chances to score.** While this formation often allows many goals to be scored against it, it also helps improve each player's abilities much faster than playing a 4-4-2 or a 5-4-1 would.

4-2-4

The 4-2-4 is a largely unused formation involving an overpowered offense, a strong defense, and large gaps in the middle of the field. The premise behind this formation is to have many attacking players (i.e., the four forwards) and many defending players (i.e., the four defenders). Since scoring and preventing the other team from scoring are the two most important objectives of most teams, this formation places players in positions to fulfill those objectives. Often, the two midfielders will be centrally located and act as holding/defensive midfielders to stop the other team's progress up the field and deliver the ball back to their forwards.

The 1970 Brazilian World Cup team won the tournament because of this formation, as well as their talented forwards who made this system effective.

3-3-4

This formation focuses on using a midfield playmaker to direct most of the attacking plays with laser-like passes and outstanding vision of the field. In the 1950s and 1960s, this was the most common formation, after the WM formation. This formation saw a small resurgence when Antonio Conte implemented it to win the Serie A with Juventus—though it could be argued that it may not have been the formation that won the Italian league, as Juventus had the best players of any team in Italy at the time. Also, Conte used this formation for the offense at Chelsea, but it resembled more of a 3-4-3 when his team was on defense.

W-M

The W-M formation essentially involves five forwards and five defenders. However, two of the forwards are on the inside right and inside left and at times double as attacking center midfielders. Also, two of the defenders act more like holding/defensive center midfielders, whose job is to stop the other team from passing and dribbling up the field.

A variation of this is the Hungarian M–U formation, in which the center forward will drop deep into the midfield to pull the center back out of position, similar to the role of the False Nine.

Therefore, it would be justifiable to call the W-M formation a kind of 3-2-5—or even a distant variation of a 3-4-3. As with any formation, how the players react to it and move will reveal its pros and cons.

In 1925, the offside rule changed the number of players needed between each team and their goal from three down to two. This change prompted the English Premier League team, Arsenal, to use the WM formation by adding more defenders to the backfield to help combat the change in rules.

2-3-5

The 2-3-5 is also known as the "inverted pyramid." Once the soccer world began to realize that passing was a more effective way to move the ball, the 2-3-5 became the standard formation. Similar to the W-M, this offense-minded formation was a result of time and what spectators considered to be a "good soccer game," which in turn influenced ticket purchases.

The 2-3-5 has two central defenders, three midfielders, and five forwards. The forwards are a left winger, an inside left, a center forward, an inside right, and a right winger.

1–2–7

This was the first standard formation used by soccer teams in England. **Prior to this formation, soccer predominately involved dribbling the ball, with passing as a last resort.** This concept was rooted in England during the 1800s and was similar to the other English sport of rugby. The single defender was known as the three-quarter-back. The two midfielders used passing to direct their team's numerous offensive players. The seven forwards were split into four wingers and three center forwards. The wingers' main task was to use their pace to collect long balls sent forward by the half-backs and three-quarter-backs, whereas the center forwards were charged with taking short passes from the wingers and were responsible for much of the goal-scoring.

Dutch Total Football

This system relied on versatile players who could attack and defend, depending on the game situation. This formation is listed as the most offensive because each player could attack. The two biggest criticisms about it were that it never won a major trophy for the Netherlands, and it required each player to be a jack of all trades, which meant they would be a master of none. Johan Cruyff, one of the best to ever play the game, was the Captain of the Dutch National Team and could effectively play in each outfield position. He was a major reason for Dutch Total Football's relative success during his career for his country.

If you look at the formations from the top of the list to the bottom, you will initially see more present-day formations with many defenders. As you travel down the list, you will notice the formations are from older generations and are considerably more offensive-minded. As you can see by the descriptions of the lesser-used formations, soccer started off as a much more offense-oriented sport. **It took almost a century for the soccer community to realize that having less than four forwards was ideal to ensure a stable defense.**

In the early days, soccer was played to win just as much as it was to be entertaining for the fans. Therefore, a formation with five attacking players on both sides resulted in many games with upwards of eight goals scored per match. During soccer's infancy, spectators were much more likely to pay for tickets when the score line included many goals, as opposed to the more familiar score lines of 1-0 for today's modern game. Soccer did not transition into a defense-first mindset for most teams until smaller nations with less talented players began to place more players in defensive positions to compete with larger nations. After all, there is some truth to the saying, "Defense wins championships."

Additionally, as with many formations mentioned in this chapter, the horizontal lines of the Big 3 formations are disappearing. **Specifically, in the old days, there were three distinct lines of players (i.e., forwards, midfielders, and defenders), but this is becoming a thing of the past.** Many modern coaches use formations that allow their players to travel between the lines, where there is considerably more space. Any of the formations in this chapter involving four numbers (e.g., the 4-1-3-2) aim to help break the three-horizontal-line mold of the Big 3 formations by giving each player on a team a more specific role on the field. In the modern soccer game, in which players' skillsets are continually becoming more advanced, using a formation that highlights each player's abilities will help ensure continued success.

Finally, understand that teams may have different formations when they are playing offense versus defense. For the most part, the positions will stay the same for nearly all players—except for one or two, who will have increased responsibilities. **These increased responsibilities are normally given to players with considerable stamina and endurance.** For example, a team attacking with a 4-3-3 formation may have a coach who asks one or both wingers to track back and create either a 4-4-2 or a 4-5-1 when their team no longer has possession of the ball.

However, a coach must recognize that having double the responsibilities is energy-consuming for a player and will require great tactical knowledge of when to travel forward versus when to hold back.

Afterword

To be a great coach, you must continue to learn, grow, and find what works best for you and your team. As the former U.S. President Harry S. Truman stated, "**Leaders are readers**." Therefore, do not stop improving your soccer knowledge, as there is a considerable amount to learn for every coach, trainer, parent, and player. You have taken the time to read this book, so you have already revealed that you likely care more and are more committed than most other coaches. Therefore, I applaud you for your efforts and want to let you know that they have not gone unnoticed.

Take the information revealed in this book to the field immediately to impact your team's game. It is not enough just to read the information; you must immediately apply it. **The trick to improvement and positive change is massive action.** Therefore, there is no better time than the present to improve your team.

If you enjoyed this book, then please leave a review on Amazon to let me know. If you learned from this book, then consider ordering a copy of the *Understand Soccer* series books *Soccer Positions* and *Soccer Dribbling & Foot Skills* to continue advancing your knowledge of this "beautiful game."

WAIT!

Wouldn't it be nice to have the steps in this book on an easy four-page printout for you to take to the field? Well, here is your chance!

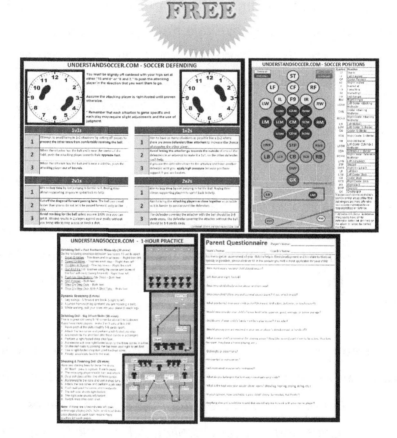

Go to this Link for an **Instant** Four-Page Printout:
UnderstandSoccer.com/free-printout

This FREE guide is simply a thank you for purchasing this book. This four-page printout will ensure that the knowledge you obtain from this book makes it to the field.

Free Book?

How would you like to obtain the next book in the series for free and have it before anyone else?

Join the Soccer Squad Book Team today and receive your next book (and potentially future books) for FREE.

Signing up is easy and does not cost anything.

Check out this website for more information:

understandsoccer.com/soccer-squad-book-team

About the Author

There he was—a soccer player who had difficulties scoring. He wanted to be the best on the field but lacked the confidence and knowledge to make his goal a reality. Every day, he dreamed about improving, but the average coaching he received, coupled with his lack of knowledge, only left him feeling alone and like he could not attain his goal. He was a quiet player, and his performance often went unnoticed.

This all changed after his junior year on the varsity soccer team at one of the largest high schools in the state. During the team-and-parent banquet at the end of the season, his coach decided to say something nice about each player. When it came to his turn to receive praise, the only thing that could be said was that he had scored two goals that season—even though it was against a lousy team, so they did not really count. It was a very painful statement: After the 20+ game season, all that could be said of his efforts were two goals that did not count.

Since that moment, he has been forever changed considering one of his greatest fears came true; he was called out in front of his family and friends. Because of that, he got serious. With a new soccer mentor, he focused on the training necessary to build his confidence and become the goal-scorer he always dreamed of being. The next season, after just a few months, he found himself in the starting position of center midfielder, and he scored his first goal of the 26-game season in only the third game.

To build his knowledge, he kept up the additional training, led by a proven goal-scorer. Fast-forward to present day, and as a result of the work he put in and by focusing on the necessary skills, he figured out how to become a goal-scorer who averages about two goals and an assist per game—all because he increased his understanding of how to play soccer. With the help of a soccer mentor, he went from being a bench-warmer who got called out in front of everybody to becoming the most confident player on the field.

Currently, he is a soccer trainer in Michigan at Next Level Training. He advanced through their rigorous program as a soccer player and was hired as a trainer. This program has allowed him to guide world-class soccer players for over a decade. He trains soccer players in formats ranging from one-hour classes to weeklong camps, and he instructs classes of all sizes, from groups of 30 to working one-on-one with individuals who want to play for the United States National Team.

If you enjoyed this book, please leave a review.

Additional Books by Dylan Joseph Available on Amazon:

Soccer Shooting & Finishing: A Step-by-Step Guide on How to Score

Soccer Dribbling & Foot Skills: A Step-by-Step Guide on How to Dribble Past the Other Team

Soccer Tryouts: A Step-by-Step Guide on How to Make the Team

Soccer Drills: A Step-by-Step Guide on How to Coach the Perfect Practice

Thank You for Reading!

Dear Reader,

I hope you enjoyed and learned from the second *Soccer Bundle* in the *Understand Soccer series*. I enjoyed writing these steps and tips to ensure you improve your game, your team's skills, or your child's abilities.

As an author, I love feedback. Candidly, you are the reason that I wrote this book and plan to write more. Therefore, I'd love to hear from you. Tell me what you liked, what you loved, and what can be improved. I'd love to hear from you. Visit UnderstandSoccer.com and scroll to the bottom of the homepage to leave me a message in the contact section or email me directly at:

Dylan@UnderstandSoccer.com

Finally, I need to ask a favor: **I'd love and appreciate a review.** As you likely know, reviews are a key part of my process to see whether you enjoyed my book. Your reviews allow me to write more books. Please take two minutes to leave a review on Amazon.com at:

https://www.amazon.com/gp/product-review/1949511170

In gratitude,

Dylan Joseph

Glossary

Note: In the *Soccer Positions* book, the term football is used interchangeably with the term soccer. Soccer is the name of the game in countries like the U.S.A, Canada, and Australia. The term football is used in Europe, the Middle East, South America, and Africa.

10 & 4 - The defensive position where your feet represent hands on a clock. Use this positioning when you want to push the attacking player to their left foot.

4-3-3 Formation - Four defenders, three midfielders, and three forwards. An offensive formation.

4-4-2 Formation - Four defenders, four midfielders, and two forwards. A standard and balanced formation.

5-4-1 Formation ("Low Block") - Five defenders, four midfielders, and one forward. A defensive formation.

8 & 2 - The defensive position where your feet represent hands on a clock. Use this positioning when you want to push the attacking player to their right foot.

50-50 - When a ball is passed into pressure or cleared up the field and your teammate and a player on the opposing team each have an equal (50%) chance of taking possession of the soccer ball.

80/20 Principle - 80% of your results come from only 20% of your actions.

Attacking Touch - Pushing the ball into space with your first touch, which is the opposite of taking a touch where the ball stops underneath you (at your feet).

Back Line - The defenders on a soccer team forming the line in front of the goalkeeper.

Ball Hawk - Someone usually close to the ball, in the right place at the right time, and a person who specializes in scoring rebounds.

Ballistic/Dynamic Stretching - Form of active movement that is not about holding a stretch but taking your body through ranges of motion that warm you up for your workout or sport. For example, shaking out your arms and performing leg swings.

Bat - The bone (hardest portion) of your foot.

Behind the Ball - When a player is between the ball and the net.

Bent/Curved Shot - A shot that spins and curves as it goes towards the net. This shot is used when you need to shoot around defenders or goalkeepers. Though you use the bone of your foot to strike the ball instead of following through the ball with your entire body, you just follow through with your leg and cross your legs after shooting the ball.

Bicycle Kick ("Overhead Kick") - where the ball is above you and you jump up and kick the ball over your body while the ball is in the air.

Big 3 Foot Skills - The jab, la croqueta, and the shot fake.

Big 3 Formations - 4-4-2, 5-4-1, and 4-3-3 formations.

Block - Deflecting or stopping the shot of an opposing player.

Brazilian League Champion - The team in the Brasileirão Serie A with the most points after their 38 games of top-flight soccer in Brazil.

Broom - In this book, it is the area on your foot towards your toes. There is space in your shoe between your toes where there is a lot more fabric and a lot less bone, which makes it a soft area on your foot, similar to the softness of a broom.

Champions League - A tournament of qualifying teams in Europe held yearly to determine who is considered the world's best club team (the European Champion). Often considered one of the top two trophies that every soccer player dreams of winning (the other being the World Cup).

Chop - This is performed with the outside of your foot. The leg that is cutting the ball must step entirely past the ball. Then, allow the ball to hit that leg/foot, which effectively stops the ball. Having the ball stop next to your foot enables the ball to be pushed in a different direction quickly.

Clearance - Kicking the ball up the field and out of pressure.

CONCACAF Cup - A soccer competition to determine CONCACAF's entry into the FIFA Confederations Cup.

Confederations Cup - An annual African club team competition. Clubs qualify for it based on their performance in their cup competitions and national leagues.

Copa América - Known as the America Cup. This is an international men's soccer competition between national teams from South America. Since 1990, there have also been teams from North America and Asia invited to participate.

Copa del Rey ("Spanish Cup") - A club competition a among 83 teams from Spain's top four flights. This is the oldest soccer competition in Spain.

Counterattack ("Fast Break") - When the team defending gains possession of the ball and quickly travels up the field with the objective of taking a quick shot, so few of the other team's players can travel back to defend in time.

Croatian Cup - The Hrvatski Nogometni Kup is a club soccer tournament in Croatia. The winner qualifies for the UEFA Europa League.

Croatian League Champion - The team in the Croatian First Football League with the most points after their 34 games of top-flight soccer in Croatia.

Crossbar Challenge - Played by one or more people where you attempt to hit the crossbar by shooting the ball from the 18-yard box.

Cruyff - Cut the ball, but leave yourself between the defender and the ball. In essence, you are cutting the ball behind your plant leg.

Cut - This is performed with the inside of your foot. The leg that is cutting the ball must step entirely past the ball. Then, allow the ball to hit that leg/foot, which effectively stops the ball. Having the ball stop next to your foot enables the ball to be pushed in a different direction quickly. Additionally, you may cut the ball so it is immediately moving in the direction you want to go.

Defender of the Year - Awarded to the player deemed the best defender in their domestic league.

Deliberate Practice - This form of practice is purposeful practice that knows where it is going and how to get there. It is guided by an understanding of what expert performers do to excel. For example, juggling with the tops of your feet towards the toes 30 times in a row to become better at settling the ball out of the air.

Driven Shot - A shot struck with the bone of your foot, where you follow through with your entire body without crossing your legs. This is the most powerful type of shot.

Dutch Cup - Known as the KNVB Cup. This club competition is amongst the top 3 flights of soccer teams in the Netherlands along with 24 other qualifying teams from lower divisions.

Dutch League Champion - The team in the Eredivisie with the most points after their 34 games of top-flight soccer in the Netherlands.

Dutch Super Cup - Known as the Johan Cruyff Shield in the Netherlands and is played by the winner of the Eredivisie (Dutch league) and the winner of the national KNVB (Dutch) Cup. If the same team wins the Eredivisie and the KNVB Cup, then that team faces the runner-up in the national league.

Dutch Total Football - A formation where no player has a set position and where each player can play in any role on the field other than goalkeeper.

Dynamic Stretching - Movement-based stretching that uses the muscles themselves to stretch other muscles. It is different from traditional "static" stretching because the stretch position is not held.

English FA Cup - English club soccer competition that is the oldest national soccer competition in the world. It is run by The Football Association.

English League Champion - The team in the English Premier League with the most points after their 38 games of top-flight soccer largely in England.

English League Cup - English club soccer competition set up by the English Football League. The 92 teams of the top four levels of English soccer battle for this cup.

FA Community Shield - English contest between the champions of the Premier League and the winners of the FA Cup. In the event they are the same team that team will play the runner-up of the league instead.

False Nine - A soccer player positioned as a center forward but plays more like an attacking midfielder to draw defenders out of the back line.

FIFA Ballon d'Or - The premier individual soccer award based on votes from international journalists and national team coaches and captains. These sources select the player who performed the best in the previous calendar year.

FIFA Club World Cup - An international men's soccer tournament, which is supposed to determine what team is the best club in the world. However, it struggles to attract interest in most of Europe and is not considered a premier trophy due to the relative strength of clubs in Europe and South America compared to the rest of the world.

FIFA Under-20 World Cup - A soccer world championship between countries occurring every two years for male players under the age of 20. Before 2006, it was known as the FIFA World Youth Championship.

Finishing - The purpose of shooting, which is to score.

Flank - The right or left sides of the field closest to the sidelines.

Flick - Barely touching the ball to change the direction of the ball slightly for a teammate when a pass is being played to you.

Footballer of the Year - Presented by the Football Writers' Association, this is an award given to the player who is voted to have the most outstanding season in English soccer that year. The winner is voted on by around 400 soccer journalists based throughout England.

Formation - The positioning of players on the field assigned by the coach.

Foundations - Passing the ball back and forth from one foot to the other using the inside of your feet.

French Cup - The Coupe de France is a French club competition run by the French Football Federation. It is open to all amateur and professional soccer clubs in France (roughly 8,500 teams), including clubs based in the overseas territories.

French League Champion - The team in the Ligue 1 with the most points after their 38 games of top-flight soccer in France.

French League Cup - The Coupe de la Ligue is a French club competition run by the Ligue de Football Professionnel. The tournament is only open to professional clubs in France which play in the country's top three soccer divisions.

French Super Cup - The Trophée des Champions is a French soccer trophy awarded to the winner of the match between the winners of the Coupe de France and the champions of Ligue 1.

Gegenpressing ("Counter-Pressing" or "6-Second Defense") - High pressure within the first six seconds of losing possession of the ball while the opponent is not set up properly to attack.

German Cup - Known as the DFB-Pokal Cup. This German soccer competition is held by the German Football Association where sixty-four club teams compete. It is considered the second-most important club title in German soccer after the Bundesliga championship.

German League Champion - The team in the Bundesliga with the most points after their 34 games of top-flight soccer in Germany.

German Super Cup - A German soccer match where the winners of the Bundesliga and the German Cup compete. It is run by the Deutsche Fußball Liga and if one team wins the Bundesliga and German Cup, they play the runner-up of the Bundesliga.

Habitual/Regular Practice - The most common form of practice where a person goes through the motions, repeating what they normally do, without being challenged or having a set goal. For example, practicing shooting from the penalty spot for fifth practice in a row.

Half-Volley - Striking the ball just after it hit the ground, but while the ball is still in the air.

High-Pressing - defending high up the pitch and inside the opposition's half. Forwards are usually the main instigators to defend far away from their own goal.

Holding Midfielder ("Defensive Midfielder") - A midfielder who sits in front of the back line and protects the center of the field.

Hyped - promote an idea or action intensively to emphasize its importance or benefits.

Interception - Stepping into a passing lane to dispossess the other team during a pass.

Intercontinental Cup - This is also referred to as the European/South American Cup. This was an official international soccer competition endorsed by UEFA and CONMEBOL between the winners of the UEFA Champions League and the South American Copa Libertadores. The competition has been replaced by the FIFA Club World Cup.

Italian Cup - The Coppa Italia is a club knockout competition in Italy. The winner qualifies for the UEFA Europa League group stage and the Supercoppa Italiana.

Italian League Champion - The team in the Serie A with the most points after their 38 games of top-flight soccer in Italy.

Italian Super Cup - An Italian soccer game played by the winners of the Serie A and the Italian Cup. If the winner of the Serie A and Italian Cup are the same team, then that team plays the Italian Cup runner-up.

Jab Step ("Feint," "Body Feint," "Fake," "Fake and Take," or "Shoulder Drop") - When you pretend to push the ball in one direction, but purposely miss, then plant with the foot that you missed the ball with to push the ball in the other direction.

Jockeying - When defending, backpedaling to maintain a proper position in relation to the person attacking with the ball. When jockeying, the defender does not dive in for the ball. He or she waits for the ideal time to steal the ball or poke it away.

Jump Turn - Instead of pulling the ball back with the bottom of your foot, as you would do in the V pull back, stop the ball with the bottom of your foot as you jump past the ball, landing with both feet at the same time on the other side of the ball. Landing with both feet at the same time on the other side of the ball allows you to explode away in the direction from which you came.

La Liga - The top-flight soccer league in Spain.

Mindset - The established set of attitudes held by someone.

MLS Cup Champion - The post-season championship game of Major League Soccer in the United States of America. This champion differs from other top soccer leagues around the world, which consider the club with the most points at the end of the regular season to be called the champion. The winner is crowned champion similar to other U.S.A. sports leagues through a playoff following a regular season.

MLS League Champion - The team in the MLS with the most points after their 34 games of top-flight soccer in the United States of America.

Offside - When you pass the ball to a player on your team who is past the opposing team's last defender at the moment the kick is initiated. You cannot be offside on a throw-in or when you are on your own half of the field.

Olympic Medalist - A gold, silver, or bronze medal is awarded to successful players at the international stage during the Olympics every four years.

One-Time Shot - When a pass or cross is played to you and your first touch is a shot on net.

Opposite Foot - Your non-dominant foot. Out of your two feet, it is the one you are not as comfortable using.

Outside of the Foot Shot ("Trivela") - Shooting with the bone of your foot where your toe is pointed down and in. The ball makes contact with the outside portion/bone of your foot. This shot is useful because it is quicker than a driven shot, it can provide bend like a bent shot, and is more powerful than a pass shot.

Park the Bus - Often, when a team has a lead, a coach will tell all their players to come back and focus almost exclusively on defense to help protect the lead

Pass Fake - Faking a pass. Keep your form the same as when you pass, including: 1) Looking at a teammate before you do a pass fake 2) Raise your passing leg high enough behind your body, so that an opponent believes you are going to kick the ball.

Pass Shot ("Finesse Shot") - A shot on the net using the inside of your foot to increase your accuracy. However, land past the ball on the follow through to increase the shot's power, similar to a shot taken with the bone of your foot.

Passing Lane - An area on the field where a teammate can pass you the ball directly, while the ball remains on the ground.

Pitch - A soccer field.

Player of the Year - The player voted as the best in their respective country's domestic soccer league that year.

Point-Man - Often a tall and strong center forward capable of winning 50-50 battles when the ball has been cleared up the field. This player's size and/or abilities help them to hold off the defenders and allow other teammates to join the attack and travel into passing lanes.

Purposeful Practice - Practice where you set specific goals for what you want to complete successfully. For example, I want to juggle the ball 30 times without letting it hit the ground.

Rainbow - When you place one foot in front of the ball and the laces of the other foot behind the ball. Pin the ball between your feet and flick the ball up behind your body and over your head.

Recovery - Intercepting a pass shortly after your team was dispossessed.

Roll ("Rollover") - Using the bottom of the toes of your foot, roll the ball parallel to the defender, crossing your feet when you plant. Then, bring your other foot around to uncross your feet and push the ball forward. The path the ball takes is the shape of an "L."

Rondo - A training game similar to "keep away" where one group of players must maintain possession of the ball by passing it around members of the opposing side.

Sandwich Feedback Technique - Give a compliment, followed by giving feedback with an explanation ended with another compliment.

Scissor - When the foot closest to the ball goes around the ball as you are attacking in a game. Emphasize turning your hips to fake the defender. To easily turn your hips, plant past the ball with your foot that is not going around the ball so that you can use the momentum of the moving ball to your advantage.

Scottish Cup - A Scottish club soccer competition for all 90 clubs of the Scottish Football Association, along with up to eight other clubs who are associate members. The Scottish Cup trophy is the oldest national trophy in the world.

Scottish League Champion - The team in the Scottish Premiership with the most points after their season of top-flight soccer in Scotland.

Scottish League Cup - Soccer competition for Scottish Professional Football League teams. The competition had a straight knockout format but was changed to a group, then knockout competition.

Self-Pass ("L," "Iniesta," or "La Croqueta") - Passing the ball from one foot to the other while running. Imagine you are doing a roll, but without your foot going on top of the ball. Instead, it is an inside of the foot pass from one foot and an inside of the foot push up the field with the other foot.

Set Piece ("Dead Ball") - A practiced plan used when the ball goes out of bounds or a foul is committed to put the ball back into play. The most common set pieces are throw-ins and free kicks.

Shielding - Placing your body between the ball and the defender. With your back facing the defender and your arms wide, prevent him or her from traveling to the ball.

Shot Fake - Faking a shot. Make sure your form looks the same as when you shoot, including: 1) Looking at the goal before you do a shot fake 2) Arms out 3) Raise your shooting leg high enough behind your body, so it looks like you will shoot.

Six-Second Defense ("Gegenpressing" or "Counter-pressing" - high-intensity pressing for the six seconds after losing possession of the ball in order to gain it back before the opposing team is in their attacking positions.

Spanish Cup - Known as the Copa Del Rey, this club competition is among 83 teams from Spain's top four flights. This is the oldest soccer competition in Spain.

Spanish League Champion - The team in La Liga with the most points after their 38 games of top-flight soccer in Spain.

Spanish Super Cup - This is known as the Supercopa de España. This contest is for Spanish soccer teams competed for by the winners of La Liga and the Copa del Rey. If the winner of La Liga and the Copa del Rey are the same team, then the winner of La Liga will play against the runner-up of the Copa del Rey.

Square to Your Teammate - Pointing your hips at a teammate.

Step On Step Out - To change direction, step on the ball with the bottom of your foot. Then, with the same foot that stepped on the ball, take another step to plant to the side of the ball, so that your other leg can come through and push the ball in a different direction.

Step Over - When you are next to the ball and you have your furthest leg from the ball step over the ball, so your entire body turns as if you are going in a completely different direction. The step over is best used along a sideline.

Sweeper - A defender that has no specific man-marking responsibilities and will often be situated behind their defending teammates to help "sweep up" any balls that travel through the defensive line.

Sweeper ("Libero" or "Free Man") - A defender that has no specific man-marking responsibilities and will often be situated behind their defending teammates to help "sweep up" any balls that travel through the defensive line.

Through Ball/Run - When a pass is played into the space in front of you, allowing you to continue your forward momentum.

Tiki-taka - high probability/short passing to help a team maintain considerable possession of the ball and frustrate the other team who is given as little as 15% time of possession.

Toe Poke/Toe Blow - Striking the ball with your big toe. The toe poke is the quickest shot, but often the most inaccurate shot.

Toe Taps - Start with the bottom of the toes of one foot on top of the ball and the other foot on the ground. Then, switch your feet so your other foot is now tapping the ball. Repeat back and forth using both feet.

Top Scorer - The soccer player who scored the most goals in their domestic league.

Treble - Achieved when a club soccer team wins three trophies in a single season. A continental treble is earned by winning the club's national league competition, the national cup competition, and a continental trophy. A domestic treble is when a team wins three national competitions. Competitions which comprise a single match (the FA Community Shield, Irish FA Charity Shield, Supercopa de España, Trophée des Champions, the Recopa Sudamericana, the UEFA Super Cup, or the Intercontinental Cup) do not count towards a treble.

UEFA Best Player in Europe - Known currently as the UEFA Men's Player of the Year Award. This soccer award is given to a soccer player on a team in Europe. Performances at the club level and for their national team are considered. UEFA created the award in 2011 to revive the Ballon d'Or, which merged with the FIFA World Player of the Year Award in 2010 to become the FIFA Ballon d'Or. This award replaced the UEFA Club Footballer of the Year award.

UEFA Champions League - A tournament of qualifying teams in Europe held yearly to determine who is considered the world's best club team (the European Champion). Often considered one of the top two trophies that every soccer player dreams of winning (the other being the World Cup).

UEFA Europa League - Previously called the UEFA Cup, this is a soccer club competition for eligible European soccer clubs. Clubs earn a place in the competition based on their performance in their national leagues and cup competitions. It ranks below the UEFA Champions League.

UEFA European Under-21 Champion - A soccer competition for men on European teams under the age of 21. This competition is held every two years.

UEFA Super Cup - A match between the UEFA Champions League and the UEFA Europa League champions.

Upper 90 - Either of the top corners on a net (corners are 90 degrees).

V Pull Back - Pull the ball backward using the bottom of your foot. Then, use your other leg to push the ball and accelerate forward in the other direction, hence the "V" in the V pull back.

Volley - Striking the ball out of the air before it hits the ground.

Wall Passing ("1-2 Passing") - A wall pass is when you pass it to a teammate and they pass it back to you with one touch similar to if you were to pass a ball against a wall.

Winger - Playing in the flanks, these attackers opposition are usually the other team's full backs. Their role is like that of outside midfielders, except these attackers play farther up the field and are expected to score significantly more than outside midfielders.

World Cup - A tournament of 32 qualifying nations from all over the world held every four years to determine which nation has the best soccer team. Often considered one of the top two trophies that every soccer player dreams of winning (the other being the Champions League).

World's Best Club Coach - Soccer award given to the most deserving club coach as voted by the International Federation of Football History & Statistics.

Acknowledgments

I would like to thank you, the reader. I am grateful to provide you value and to help you on your journey of becoming a more confident soccer player, coach, or parent. I am happy to serve you and thank you for the opportunity to do so. Also, I would like to recognize people that have made a difference and have paved the way for me to share this book with you:

First, I want to thank my mother who has been a role model for what can be done when you work hard towards your goals. Her work ethic and ability to overcome adversity are truly admirable, and I look up to her for this.

Second, I would like to thank the editors Abbey Decker, Kevin Solorio, Kimberly Stewart, Paul Marvar, Toni Sinistaj, and Youssef Hodroj. They reviewed this book for areas that could be improved and additional insights to share. Without their input, this book would not be the high-quality reading material you have come to expect in the *Understand Soccer* series.

Lastly, I would like to thank my soccer trainer, Aaron Byrd, whose wisdom and smarts have turned me into the player I am today. His guidance and knowledge about this game have made it so that I can pass this knowledge on to rising stars, coaches looking to grow their understanding of soccer, and caring parents!

Many thanks,

Dylan Joseph

Made in the USA
Las Vegas, NV
03 April 2024